Between Hope & Despair

Between Hope & Despair

Women Learning Politics

Donna M. Chovanec

Fernwood Publishing • Halifax and Winnipeg

To Tito
por la conciencia

Editing: Jean Wilson
Cover design: John van der Woude
Printed and bound in Canada by Hignell Book Printing
Printed on paper containing 100% post-consumer fibre.

Published in Canada by Fernwood Publishing
32 Oceanvista Lane
Black Point, Nova Scotia, B0J 1B0
and #8–222 Osborne Street, Winnipeg, Manitoba, R3L 1Z3
www.fernwoodpublishing.ca

Fernwood Publishing Company Limited gratefully acknowledges the financial support
of the Government of Canada through the Book Publishing Industry Development
Program (BPIDP), the Canada Council for the Arts and the Nova Scotia
Department of Tourism and Culture for our publishing program.

Library and Archives Canada Cataloguing in Publication

Chovanec, Donna M.
Between hope and despair: women learning politics / Donna M.
Chovanec.

Includes bibliographical references.
ISBN 978-1-55266-299-1

1. Women in politics—Chile—Arica—Case studies.
2. Women—Chile—Arica—Social conditions—Case studies. 3. Social
movements—Chile—Arica—Case studies. 4. Chile—Politics and
government—1973- —Case studies. I. Title.

HQ1236.5.C5C56 2009   303.48'40820983123   C2008-907768-7

Contents

Acknowledgements

First, to Héctor González for being the impetus behind the research contained in this book and for accompanying me on this journey from the beginning. Also for his invaluable research assistance during the periods of fieldwork — connecting me to participants, clarifying language and cultural nuances, translating and facilitating. But above all, for being the person who awakened my political consciousness.

Miles de gracias to many people who helped me, each in their own way, with the fieldwork in Chile. To the many women in Arica who accepted me in their lives, told me their stories and shared with me the joy and pain guarded deep in their memories. I hope that the words written in these pages resonate for them as echoes of their courageous struggle. To the team at Casa de Encuentro de la Mujer (CEDEMU) — Berta Moreno (director), Sandra Bravo, Marianella González and Lorena Ríos — who warmly welcomed me and included me as part of the team during my stay in Arica. Especially to Berta and Sandra for being, on top of everything else, good and very patient friends. Also to Carmen Fuentes, the previous director of CEDEMU, who initially facilitated my request to work with CEDEMU on this project. To the various members of Movimiento por los Derechos de la Mujer (MODEMU) who shared their memories and their archives with me. To Magaly Ortíz for professionally transcribing countless hours of interviews. To the librarians at the Santiago office of ISIS International for helping me locate relevant reports and articles. To Susan Franceschet, now a professor at the University of Calgary, for her valuable assistance in preparing me for the fieldwork, for sharing her references and for introducing me to useful resources in Chile.

I also extend my deepest appreciation to many who helped me during my graduate program. To my doctoral supervisor, Marilyn Assheton-Smith, who waited patiently through the ups and downs of my progress, believed in me and steadfastly guided me toward completion. To Sue M. Scott, my co-supervisor, who first introduced me to "adult education for social change" two decades ago, actively nurtured my academic development and stimulated my passion for research. I thank her most especially for her friendship and her faith in me. To my colleagues in Research Services at the Alberta Alcohol and Drug Abuse Commission (AADAC) who consistently supported me in so many ways while I was working on my doctoral program, especially to Art Dyer, Z'Anne Harvey Jansen, Kathy Huebert and Susan Hart.

To my fellow graduate students and dear friends who keep me grounded and connected. To Sue Brigham, Gloria Filax and Jennifer Kelly. To the Wings Women — Karen Barnes, Pauline Collette, Kathy Dowding, Maureen Konrad and Carrie Saylor. To all the members of Club IDC (International Development Concerns), now dispersed across the globe.

To Alexandra Benitez for her valuable partnership over the past three years in researching and writing about the Penguin Revolution in Chile and to the funding provided by the Roger Smith Undergraduate Research Award for her assistance.

To friends and colleagues at the University of Alberta who provided feedback on versions of this manuscript, especially to Elizabeth Lange, Ali Abdi, Rene Leiva and my students in a course on social movement learning.

I could not have done this project without generous financial support. For this, I am most grateful for the following: International Development Research Centre Doctoral Research Award, Izaak Walton Killam Memorial Scholarship, Organization of American States PRA Fellowship, Social Sciences and Humanities Research Council Doctoral Fellowship, University of Alberta Dissertation Fellowship, Province of Alberta Graduate Fellowship and also for internal awards granted to faculty at the University of Alberta that allowed me to conduct the most recent research.

Most importantly, endless love and gratitude to my family. To Amalia González Chovanec, who, as a youngster, walked with me every step of the way through the months of fieldwork and the long days and nights of writing. To Esteban, Carolina and Alejandra González — young Chilean exiles and my stepchildren — whose lives are a testament to the despair and hope revealed within these pages. To my mother, Minnie Chovanec, and my siblings, Carol and Robert, for helping me whenever and however I needed it through the long years of study. Especially to my Mom, who taught me to believe in myself and to care about other people.

Introduction

The women were the first to organize in Chile for the need to be united. Fundamentally, to defend the family, to defend the children, to defend life; because they had no food, because their husbands didn't have work, because they didn't have a lot of things. So, they united to be able to do things... From the roots of this we saw emerging, not a tiny organization, but a more massive one. And the women organized public demonstrations, not only to be united but also to go out into the street with strength. The first demonstrations in Chile against the dictatorship were done by women. So, they initiated the road to the end of the dictatorship to be able to say to the government, to the military, that despite everything they had done to restrict liberty, the women could do things anyway. And they demonstrated in the street that, yes, you can break what the military had tried to carry out. You see? They went out and no one could stop them. (participant in the women's movement in Arica, Chile)

I don't know how it happened that I grew into adulthood not knowing anything about Chile's dictatorship or the courageous women and men, young and old, who struggled against it. How is it possible that we can live *in* the world, be *of* the world but know so little *about* the world?

This book is one account of the many stories of the women's movement in Chile as it has unfolded over the past decades. It is an empirical account of political learning in social movements through the study of the women's movement in Arica, a small city in Chile's northern frontier. My partner, Héctor González, a Chilean-in-exile, was raised in Arica. He was only ten years old on September 11, 1973 — the day of the military coup in Chile. Along with countless others, he spent his adolescence struggling against the dictatorship. As he shared his memories with me, I was outraged by the injustices he recounted yet captivated by the bravery of the anti-dictatorship activists, especially those in the women's movement. During a visit to Chile in 1993, Héctor introduced me to some of these women. As an adult educator concerned about social justice and social change, this compelling experience prompted me to focus my doctoral research on exploring the women's political learning and drawing attention to the educational processes at work within the women's movement.

Therefore, in 2001–2, I conducted fieldwork in Arica. During that time, I lived in a working-class neighbourhood with Héctor and my four-year-old daughter, fourteen-year-old stepson, and at different intervals, with members of the extended family. Living in Arica as a family with ties to the community and to the past allowed me to participate as a neighbour, as a mother and as the spouse of a citizen of Arica, but with the distinctive status accorded to a Canadian researcher. In this context, buying bread, talking to neighbours, watching television news, participating in social events and many more daily activities were continuous sources of new learning. The fieldwork was further facilitated through my connection with Casa de Encuentro de la Mujer (CEDEMU), a community-based women's non-governmental organization (NGO) that served as my field base. Although CEDEMU was facing a number of organizational changes at the time, the team of four women welcomed me warmly and provided assistance in multiple ways. Working in Spanish with the collaboration of CEDEMU and local research assistants, I interviewed over fifty women, aged twenty-five to seventy-eight, who had been active in social and political movements in Arica during the previous thirty years; all were activists in the anti-dictatorship struggle during the 1980s. In individual and group interviews, we asked the women to recount their involvement in social and political movements and to describe what and how they learned from those experiences. (See Chapter 5 for more detail on the research methods.)

I returned to Chile to share findings and gather information just before the 2006 election of Chile's first woman president, Michele Bachelet. Later in the same year, a new generation of activists exploded on the scene in Chile, prompting me to revisit my earlier findings about learning in the women's movement. Since then, I have been monitoring media and other electronic literature on the student movement in Chile, complemented by an exploratory interview with two student movement leaders in Arica in 2007.

Why Study Political Learning in the Women's Movement?

Some of the most powerful learning occurs as people struggle against oppression, as they struggle to make sense of what is happening to them and to work out ways of doing something about it. (Foley 1999: 1–2)

It is this kind of "powerful learning" that inspires my interest in social movements. Social movements are distinct forms of collective action that include political or cultural conflicts, informal networks and a collective identity (della Porta and Diani 2006). Reading between the lines of any account of a social movement, it is clear that political learning is a significant component of activism. Activists continuously and dialectically learn and teach throughout social action. Rarely, however, do social movement scholars explicitly study this pedagogical dimension.

There are exceptions. Along with other scholars in the field of adult education, I have been studying the learning dimension of social movements for almost twenty years. In an earlier project, I explored how abused women learned their way out of victimization to become survivors and then advocates in the struggle against violence against women (Chovanec 1994). The women's journey included a consciousness-raising process that incorporated personal, social and action elements in an abused women's program. The program had three educational segments: two that focused on personal development and a theoretical understanding of abuse as a social issue, and a third that was oriented to change strategies such as personal and public advocacy.

I asked more or less the same question about the anti-dictatorship women's movements in Chile: How did women learn their way out of victimization to become oppositional activists against the dictatorship? More specifically, I asked: What are the methods (processes and content) of political learning within the social movement? How are knowledge and skills transmitted through social movement participation? What is the relationship of these processes to social change? How could the study of political learning in the powerful women's movement in Arica provide inspiration and strategies for social movements throughout the world? This book addresses these questions.

Outline of the Book

Part 1 of this book, the Arica Story, is told through the women's words and experiences. In Chapter 1, I review the setting and the context, incorporating literature about the socio-political situation in Chile. In Chapter 2, I examine some of the familial and social factors that are precursors to the women's activism. In Chapter 3, the women tell the story of their own powerful anti-dictatorship activism, from the inception of the women's movement in Arica to the end of the dictatorship and installation of the newly elected president in 1990. They describe their multiple roles and activities as well as their own learning experiences and the emotions that accompany them. Chapter 4 covers the period from 1990 to the present, in which the women vacillate between despair and hope as they consider both the past and the future. In this chapter, I also introduce the newest generation of political actors, the adolescent descendents of the anti-dictatorship struggle.

In Part 2, I focus on the political learning and educational processes at work in the women's movement. After providing an overview of the research study including theory, context and methods in Chapter 5, I look at three key learning themes that emerged from the narrative in Part 1. These themes are: political consciousness (Chapter 6), social movement praxis (Chapter 7) and how participating in social movements changes lives (Chapter 8). In the final chapter, I consider the role of the adult educator in social movements.

Terms and Translations

Before proceeding, it is important to clarify the following:

- All translations from transcripts and original sources in Spanish are mine. Unless otherwise indicated, text in quotation marks is from interviews with the women. "The women" refers to the women who participated in the research study.
- In Spanish, all nouns have a feminine or masculine modifier. When the noun is intended to represent both genders, the masculine modifier is typically used to signify gender neutrality. Following feminists in Chile, I use both modifiers so that both genders are more clearly included, for example, *pobladores/as*.
- "Pinocho" is the Spanish word for Pinocchio and is a derogatory reference to

the Chilean dictator, General Augusto Pinochet.

- I use the word "popular" as it is used in critical discourse. Derived from the root word *pueblo* (people), "popular" and its derivatives connote something related to the poor and working-class sectors. For example, a *población* is a neighbourhood where *pobladores/as*, poor and working-class people, live.

- All photos but one are from my personal collection of photos that were given to me by various members of the activist community in Arica. The photo in Chapter 4 entitled "Students protest outside the cathedral, June 6, 2006" is used with permission from the photographer, Rodrigo Achá, who posted the photo on flickr®.

Part 1
The Arica Story

1

Introduction

The Scene: It is October 29, 1983. On this evening, one by one and in silence, about sixty women surreptitiously enter a senior citizens' centre in the small city of Arica in northern Chile. What brings these women together? Have they not noticed that it is past curfew? Have they forgotten that it is illegal to meet in groups of more than three? Surely, after ten years of a brutal military dictatorship they must know the risk they are taking.

What prompts them, then, to come together in this clandestine and dangerous fashion? The answer to this question is both simple and complex. In its most uncomplicated form, the answer might be *"es necesario"* — it is necessary. But what makes it necessary? How and why and for whom is it necessary? What response is demanded by this deceptively simple imperative?

To glimpse the depth of the response needed for these questions requires a journey from the past to the present that showcases the bravery of elders and the commitment of contemporaries: a journey in which marches hold maternal rather than military significance, in which the very private and domestic act of cooking is a public act of defiance, in which balaclavas offer flimsy protection, not from a bitter wind but from a cruel torturer, in which the sanctity of the church becomes the sanctuary of the community and in which the university is more often a site of clashes than classes.

While the women have different interpretations of what happened at this meeting in 1983, it is clear that it was a pivotal moment in the trajectory of the women's movement in Arica. The meeting signalled the birth of the second wave of the women's movement in Arica and set the stage for the future of the movement.

After an introduction to the setting and the context, the Arica Story is told in four parts, each part like an act in a play. In Act I, I reveal Los Antecedentes, the family and social environments in which the women were raised and that contributed to their later activism. Act II is La Lucha — the struggle — where I chronicle the myriad activities and experiences of the women's movement in Arica during the anti-dictatorship struggle, from the meeting in 1983 to the end of the dictatorship in 1990. This hitherto "unwritten" story of these women is a tribute to their bravery, their commitment, their growth, their losses, their triumphs and their failures. In Act III, the women integrate an astute analysis of the demobilization and institutionalization of the women's movement in Chile with their own poignant emotional responses. Here, I also introduce the newest generation of political actors in Chile, Los Pingüinos — the Penguins. These descendants of the anti-dictatorship struggle began mobilizing in 2006 against the lingering neo-liberal legacy of the dictatorship in the educational system in Chile. Their massive protests have sparked a broad-based movement demanding extensive political changes.

To remember, to honour, to thank, to cry and maybe to laugh — this is their story.

The Setting

The setting is the city of Arica, Chile's most northern outpost, more than 2000 km from the capital city of Santiago. Situated along the Pacific Ocean at the crossroads of Peru, Bolivia and Chile, this borderland community has been shaped by territorial battles over many centuries. Arica is a coastal city of 180,000 people, capriciously carved out of the driest desert in the world at the foot of the Andes Mountains, crafting a fusion of sand, sea and sky that incongruously spawns fertile valleys unexpectedly appearing throughout the surrounding countryside. Arica stubbornly preserves many aspects of its heritage, demonstrated in the lifestyle of the people and the customs of the community. The cultural identity of the city is richly patterned by the indigenous people of Inca ancestry, the Aymara and the Quechua, who traditionally have lived in the *altiplanos* (highlands) high above Arica where llamas and their kin graze on vast plateaus. Although it is slowly changing, people still organize their daily routine according to the traditional large mid-day meal and siesta, and hundreds of people attend cultural festivals in the streets.

Walking along the main downtown street closed to traffic, one sees dogs running loose everywhere and all kinds of people — men in business suits, women in the uniform of their company, children in school uniforms and gypsies in traditional clothing engaged in the very non-traditional act of begging. How the economy operates in Arica is transparent on that one downtown street. There are no shopping malls filled with transnational retail outlets; one struggling McDonald's is the only transnational food chain in Arica. There is a national or transnational private bank on every corner. There are small businesses selling clothing or household appliances, restaurants of every size and kind, and micro-businesses operating out of tiny kiosks selling newspapers and candy. The informal (underground) economy is evident in the abundance of desperate vendors, mostly women sitting with their young children on the sidewalk, selling gum, aspirin or anything else that might earn them a *peso* that day. There is also a whole area of talented local artisans and musicians just off the main street.

In the *poblaciones*, houses are connected one to the other in block-long rows, each one vastly different from the other, divulging the economic means of its occupants. The houses are made for dry, rainless weather, their flat rooftops serving as storage areas. Every corner boasts a *peluquería* (hair salon) and a small store with a handwritten sign announcing "*hay pan,*" meaning that the delicious fresh Chilean bread has arrived. Greeting folks and meeting new people is done with a *beso* (kiss) on the cheek. No one hurries. There is always another bus or *colectivo* (shared taxi) and a friend or colleague happy to see you whenever you get there. Summer days are spent on the many beaches in the city, and summer evenings are passed at the ocean-side park where the promenade and playground play host to concerts, frolicking children and mothers pushing strollers.

Prior to 1973, Arica was a socially and economically thriving community, but after the military coup, it became a highly militarized and economically depressed zone. In many *poblaciones*, problems with drugs and crime are evident and there are few recreational or social outlets for youth. Like many cities around the world, Arica is a city of contrasts and contradictions. But here, as elsewhere in the global south, they are more pronounced than a just world should allow. Here, they exist precisely because an unjust world does allow it.

The Context

Five centuries of European colonization have left enduring and devastating cultural and economic imprints in Latin America and have effectively paved the way for twentieth-century neo-colonial domination: development, modernization and globalization. During the inauguration of the neo-liberal era, Latin America's position in the global hierarchy was solidified by a dual reign of terror — brutally repressive military regimes in combination with a crippling monetarist economic model. During the 1960s and '70s, many countries in the region were forcibly overtaken and governed by right-wing military dictatorships. The few countries with socialist governments faced externally generated anti-government propaganda or direct obstruction of internal policies.

Unlike many of its neighbours, Chile had a long and stable social democratic tradition that resulted in the election of a socialist president, Salvador Allende, in 1970. The socialist experiment, however, proved too threatening for both national and international powers. Aided by internal agitation by the upper class and the involvement of the United States (Chavkin 1985), in 1973 a military coup d'état under the direction of General Augusto Pinochet overthrew the government and installed a military dictatorship. Immediately thereafter, the constitution was suspended, the media was censured and political parties and trade unions were prohibited. During the bloody early days of the coup, thousands were captured, detained, tortured, "disappeared" or executed. Over 3000 people were assassinated by the Chilean state during the dictatorship years, more than 1000 of whom remain disappeared. Political leaders, community organizers, labour activists and intellectuals who escaped this fate were forced into hiding while the rest of the citizenry was paralyzed by fear. "Five million women survived with the most profound fear on their shoulders." About one million Chilean women were exiled and 500,000 children were born in exile.[1]

Repression of the citizenry established the climate needed to experiment with rapid economic restructuring without worrying about the destabilizing tendency of popular political activity (Craske 1998). Based solidly in the emerging neo-liberal economic model, the Chilean military regime applied international guidelines for a market economy within the first years of the coup (Chavkin 1985; Silva 1991) and then, in the 1980s, instituted externally imposed structural adjustment policies (SAPS). As a result of the reduction and privatization of government services mandated by these policies (among other requirements), there was a 27 percent reduction in the public budget in Chile (Schuurman 1993), exacerbating the already extreme poverty around the country. The harsh economic measures consolidated neo-liberalism in the region, escalating economic hardship for increasing numbers of citizens and fundamentally changing the social structure of the family and the society.

Although Chile's history of oppression is strong, so too is its history of resistance and dissent. The region has a vibrant history of trade unionism and of women's, workers', peasants', and indigenous people's movements. Although these movements were immobilized and then forced underground during the first years after the coup in Chile, "during the early 1980s social movements reemerged and formed the backbone of the popular protest movement" (Hipsher 1996: 280–81). The years 1980 to 1989 witnessed various collective responses to economic and human rights abuses, including the outbreak of organized mass protests across all sectors of Chilean society. The first National Day of Protest occurred on May 11, 1983, followed by the first mass mobilization of the women's movement against the dictatorship on August 11, 1983. Paradoxically, the political mobilization of Chilean women increased sharply in the 1980s in the midst of state repression and coincident with the emergence of second-wave feminism (see, for example, Baldez 2002; Chuchryk 1989; Franceschet 2005; Gaviola, Largo and Palestro 1994; Schild 1994; Valdés and Weinstein 1993).

While most Latin American dictatorships dissolved for various reasons during the early 1980s, the Chilean military government outlasted all others. When a plebiscite dictated by Pinochet's own 1980 constitution was called in 1988, a broad-based coalition of anti-dictatorship groups successfully waged a campaign to vote against continued military rule. This obliged Pinochet to hold elections in 1989 after seventeen years as dictator. A coalition of centre-left parties, the Concertación por la Democracia, initially negotiated the terms of transfer to civil rule and won the election.

Throughout Latin America, the period after the downfall of a dictatorship was known as the "transition to democracy" — a time during which electoral processes and political parties were gradually re-established. Chile's transition period began in 1990. In the early days of the transition, the new government was hampered by a combination of anxiety about the potential for a renewed military takeover and the negotiated terms of the transition. In order to secure a stable transition to democracy, the economy was prioritized and social justice demands were put on hold (Craske 1998). However, after four subsequent elections all won by the Concertación, there is growing pessimism about the political will of this government to address the negative consequences of over thirty years of neo-liberal policies or to consolidate a true democracy in Chile. (See Bresnahan 2003 for a discussion of the adverse effects of neo-liberal economics on the democratization process in Chile.)

Note

1. The Agrupación de Familiares de Detenidos Desaparecidos de Chile published the statistics in this paragraph. The numbers are drawn from the government reports produced by the National Truth and Reconciliation Commission (Rettig Report) and the National Corporation for Reconciliation and Reparation. Similar statistics were published in the *Washington Post* (2000). While statistics differ across sources, most agree that the available numbers are an underestimate of the true extent of the tragedy.

2

Act I — Los Antecedentes (The Antecedents)

On the Path to Socialism: Pre-1973

Prior to the military coup in 1973, women who would later become activists in the anti-dictatorship struggle in Arica were being raised in family and social environments that espoused a democratic and socialist worldview predicated upon their unique northern history, religious or family values, political party affiliation and/ or the socialist era.

Many of these women could claim *obrero* (worker), *campesino* (peasant) or *salitrero* (nitrate miner) origins, especially those women whose personal stories are situated within the long history of territorial battles and conquered people over many centuries in the Chilean north. Women activists in Arica are aware of the legacy of struggle within the mining communities of the north, where women and children protested and sometimes died alongside their husbands and fathers for condemning the oppressive and repressive treatment of workers at the hands of the mining companies. The popular Chilean musical production, La Cantata Santa María de Iquique, chronicles the tragic story of 20,000 marchers — men, women and children — from the northern mining communities who arrived in Iquique in 1907 to protest their unjust working and wretched living conditions. Many were shepherded into the courtyard of La Escuela Santa Maria, where authorities opened fire. Fifteen hundred were massacred.[1] Some of the elder women in this study had roots in *la pampa* (the desert), in communities such as Chuquicamata, whose distinctive history is responsible for the "politicization" of the north. As described by one of these women:

> There is something to mention that is very important for the Chilean movements. All that culture that there was, that politicization that there was, that effervescent social thing that there was, wasn't because the Chilean people were tough. No. It was because in our history there was a very important man, Luis Emilio Recabarren … who organized the workers for their rights in the north. Then others followed. But all of it relates to the repression of the miners … Therefore … it was an organization that came from much before, the politicization and the organization of the Chilean people.

Some women were raised in environments where values such as solidarity or reciprocity were expressed in everyday actions, as in this quote from a woman who for many years was the director of an NGO in one of the poorest *poblaciones* in Arica.

It's true that my family wasn't one with a lot of political consciousness, but it was one with a lot of consciousness of values. My father and my mother [were] a white man and an indigenous woman ... I saw that many people arrived at my house, people from the rural area, indigenous people, very poor people, prostitutes, beggars. Many people entered my house. So therefore, the values of solidarity were recurring values. I mean, there were many people who came to my house, who entered and then left with no problem. So, I have this, like, very ingrained in me. For me, it's like there was always the sense of being able to see beyond the person. There was always the sense of reciprocity, quite strongly, and of appreciating [people's] worth. My father saw someone that didn't have shoes to put on and my father gave him his sandals... And on top of that, my mother is a woman of indigenous origin, humble but with much faith ... in people and in God and in la Pacha [the Earth].

Most of the women were explicitly exposed to communism or socialism in the course of their families' participation in a political party. "*Desde la cuna*" (from the cradle) or "*en la sangre*" (in the blood), these women learned their philosophies and politics through their earliest childhood experiences.

I come from a family of socialists... Always in my house the environment was a socialist environment. Therefore, very early I started to participate. First, when I was a little girl, so as not to leave me alone in the house, they took me to the meetings of the party.

A few women, daughters of communist parents who fled to the north of Chile from Santiago in order to escape an earlier period of political repression, were deeply affected by this childhood experience. "In the era of the government of the traitor González Videla, my parents were communist militants. So from very young, I began to know what it meant to live violently uprooted. Unconsciously, [my sister and I] found ourselves involved in the subject [of politics]."[2]

Some women listed a variety of leftist parties to which a host of family members belonged. In some cases, it was a long-standing family tradition to belong to a particular political party.

I am from a family that no one can be from another party because everyone is communist and we have all the generations, all, all, all of them are the same. And if someone marries someone who isn't, they are obligated to convert and those that don't, leave. Get it? It's like a clan.

Moving into the second half of the twentieth century, citizens of Arica were benefiting from the growing ascendancy of the left in municipal government, in the consolidation of communitarian projects, in a healthy labour movement and in a thriving industrial, agrarian and mining-based economy. These benefits were collectively shared through initiatives such as the Junta de Adelanto de Arica (Arica Council of Progress) that over a twenty-year period accomplished numerous social and economic development projects in housing, education and commercial construction (Universidad de Chile 1972). The women provided many examples of active democratic citizen participation at the community level, especially in the *juntas de vecinos* (neighbourhood councils) and the *centros de madres* (mother's centres), two of the most prominent and active grassroots citizens' organizations. *Tomas de terreno* (land takeovers), a legacy from earlier decades, were common as people from all over the country arrived in Arica, a city unable to keep up with the housing demands of a growing population of "*inmigrantes internos*" (internal immigrants). A woman describes the actions involved in a land takeover:

> The problem was that I didn't have anywhere to live... Well, the *tomas de terreno* emerged. A man offered to give my husband a piece of land in [a *población* in Arica] but we had to take it clandestinely because it was the only way to live in 1958... So this is how we began to do the *tomas de terreno*. In one night, we would take, for example, five or six different *poblaciones*... At 3:00 in the morning, we put up the plywood, we put a flag on a pole, and we set everything down... Then all the cops came there... And that is what the struggle for the *pobladores* is all about, the *toma de terreno*. There was no water, there was no electricity, there was no sewer system.

Through their community organizations, the *pobladores/as* later negotiated with the authorities to formally obtain the land and establish services in the community.

Then, in 1970, the Unidad Popular (Popular Unity) government, a coalition led by socialist president Salvador Allende, was elected. Women who were children and adolescents in 1970 recalled the happiness, hope and solidarity of the Allende years. "I was little," began one woman "we all went to raise the flag. It was the popular government, it was the hope of my family — that for four [times] had voted for Allende — with a sense that this is the government of the poor, this is *our* government." Older women had often worked for Allende's successive campaigns:

> I participated actively, I mean actively, in the Unidad Popular government and not only in the government but much before as well. Here we talk of four periods before Allende assumed power. I was involved in this, struggling so that our people would have real justice, that there would be equality, [because] there were so many things, scarcities that our people had.[3]

Women remembered the community programs and the community spirit. "The effervescence of the youth, the voluntary work, the summer work, the summer camps were realities... that we joyously lived." They remembered that "everyone participated, everyone had a job, any little job, in the neighbourhood." As right-wing opposition to the Allende government escalated over his three-year presidency, communitarian responses increased in an effort to provide mutual support and to circumvent the anti-government propaganda and boycotts. For example, *juntas de abastecimiento y precios* (councils of supplies and prices) were established and charged with obtaining and fairly distributing food during the food shortages that were contrived by forces opposed to the Allende government.[4] A teacher in the Brigade of Socialist Teachers was responsible for distributing meat:

> I had an agreement [with the meat market] and I arrived every Friday with my little box. And I gave a half a kilo of meat to everyone… as a way to have the people more or less provided for. And to be able to placate the situation a little because we knew that they were creating an environment for the people to reject the government more and more.

Throughout Latin America, Catholic doctrine during the age of liberation theology in the 1970s was a powerful educational tool through formal workshops and informal solidarity. One woman explained this influence:

> When I was a bit older, I began to see things. I began to realize what they were talking about, of what religion must be, that it is for everyone to be equal… What was important was that supposedly in the church we were all children of God, that everyone had the same rights. And I began to, like, see the ideal that one has. I mean, they preached about equality before the eyes of God, that we are all equal. And the priest and the nun, in the political part, also told you that we are all equal. I mean, before the society, we all have to be equal… For me, it was very important, very, very important.

From One Day to the Next: September 11, 1973

Regardless of their age on September 11, 1973, women clearly remember what they were doing on the day of the coup, the day when their lives were suddenly turned upside down. Girls were playing in the streets, housewives and mothers were going about their daily routine of shopping for groceries or walking children to school, and teachers were starting their classes. The women recalled not only what was happening on that fateful day but also how they felt: bewildered, frightened and stunned. One woman remembered the day of the coup from her perspective as a child. From the freedom to play in the streets to suddenly being confined to the back of the house, the child understood that "something was happening":

> I was eight or nine years old, but I remember my house. Obviously, it was just like children to go out to play in the street. But from one day to the next, the curtains were closed in my house and we were not permitted to enter any of the front part of the house, not the living room, dining room or front hall. My father closed those parts. What's more, he put a lock on that part because of the shooting that was happening in the middle of the night. I'm talking about September 11 in the night and September 12. Nobody explained anything to me. I came to understand it much later. I

felt the shots. I felt that something was happening because [normally] we went to bed at 12 and now, at 6 or 7 in the evening, the lights were turned off in the house. It was a very sudden thing, very, very sudden.

A mother poignantly conveys the drastic change in her life in the small space of time between taking her children to school and returning home.

Look, so that you understand and can comprehend better, it is like you wake up one particular day to do your everyday things, as happened to me, for example. You wake up in the morning and I had to take my children to school, it was the little ones that I had to take. When I returned from the school, there my life changed. For me, it changed totally. When I saw nobody in the street, only military vehicles, tanks, trucks full of military all painted up, with machine guns. I mean, that occupation of the city was such a terrible thing … That change, so sudden, was so terrible.

Although there had been growing unrest throughout the country, especially in the capital city, the contra-Allende faction in Arica was quite small, likely due to the established leftist consciousness and practices in the city. "The demonstrations, the protests of women, the line-ups [for food], no, not here like in Santiago. [The support for Allende] was very strong here. The left was always very strong here." Thus, women in Arica, even those who were political leaders and party militants, were completely stunned by the coup. A woman who was the mayor of Arica at the time remembered, "We had no idea that there was going to be a military coup. I arrived at work… like always before 8:00… and at 10 they took me into detention from there." The reality of new dangers was brought home to one *pobladora* on the first day of the coup:

I am very patriotic so my first reaction was to [put up] a flag and black crepe at half-mast because [President Allende] had died. Well, the flag was raised for a few hours and a young man went by, running desperately over here and he stopped at the house and entered and he said to me, "Señora, please take down the flag." And I said, "I'm not going to take down the flag because the President of the Republic has died, they killed him."… The young man climbed up and took down the black crepe and continued running. I never knew who he was, and well, it was really terrible. I don't know, maybe that young man saved me from many things because after that I knew that other *poblaciones*… did the same. The military came and struck the housewives.

Some, although shaken, were confident that the traumatic disruption would quickly pass. "[Some people] thought this would only last a while and afterwards the military would give back the power — that didn't happen." A woman who was a Communist Party leader at the time described the personal and political effect of the coup.

The coup caught me by surprise. It was such a mess. What happened? We were not sure of what had happened. With so much fear, four months pregnant, not knowing what to do, I was sorry that I was pregnant because we thought — I talked with my husband, and we said that it was crazy to be pregnant in these times … because we thought that there was going to be a response from the people and that people would be needed. I don't know if it was a relief or a great disappointment to see that there was no kind of response. In Arica, the response was minimal; the response to the coup was minimal … The coup arrived and left us hanging, politically. Nothing happened. We had no contact with anybody for a long time. We came to know that people had been taken to prison. We tried to listen to Radio Moscow every night to have some news, without knowing, without being able to communicate with my family in Santiago either.

Many women sadly recognized the irreversible effect that this day had on the rest of their lives, collectively and personally. In the women's words, "the future that might have been" was shattered "from one day to the next — everything, everything, all your dreams, your family … there is a 100 degree turn." "From September 11, 1973, it was an absolutely different world." "Life changed in that moment and for every moment after." Another woman and her husband lost their jobs. For them, "from one day to the next without a salary, without a home, without a job, I mean, that meant a mental re-adaptation."

From there, the story is familiar:

Everyone knows now about the overthrow and, at the same time, the death [of Allende] … the torture, arbitrary detentions, deaths, disappearances — children, husbands, siblings, friends that were lost and disappeared. And still today, for many of them, the family has not received an answer.

The days and months changed to years in which every day was infused with terror.

I grew up in a regimen of fear… I have memories that stand out. Tanks were outside my house, you know, and the military shooting. So, even if you don't want to be involved, it frightens you anyway. You are frightened that they will take your parents to prison. You are frightened that a relative of yours has been taken to prison when you see that the military had arrived. And they took your neighbours and you witnessed that and you're praying that they don't touch your parents tomorrow. So all those things are affecting you.

Quiet Continuity: 1973–83

Immediately after the coup, all forms of social and political movements were "disarticulated." In Arica, there were many reasons for this. One reason was fear. Because one's friends either "*se fueron or las fueron*" (left or were taken away), "your whole social circle was dismantled." Many women felt distrust and suspicion, afraid to talk to anyone for not knowing who was an informant. "Even to greet a person was suddenly dangerous." Consequently, people tried "to pass by unnoticed ... [and] as discreetly as possible." For a time, this kept the women isolated and silent. "A while passed without doing anything outside my home, I mean, nothing political, nothing social."

A second reason for the disintegration of social movements was that the conspicuous militarization of the city acted as a form of insidious surveillance. Not only was there a large "amount of people that were in regiments in Arica at that time" but also, according to one leader, the military infiltrated the neighbourhoods.

> As a frontier city, the dictatorship had a different characteristic here. From my point of view, it was a city militarily surrounded. And how did they surround us? They surrounded us by putting people in the *poblaciones*, soldiers, military, in the *poblaciones*. For every two or three houses, one was a house of a military. In this way, they neutralized the neighbourhood. They kept an eye on everything and knew everything that happened in the *población*.

The third reason was that women were overloaded with all the tasks of managing things alone because men, the traditional family breadwinners, were unemployed. Many had to leave Arica to work elsewhere, usually in the mining communities, and "for the first time, women, housewives, mothers, had to abandon their homes, so to speak, to go out to work." Another woman, formerly very active in social and political activities, said, "I was left with little time to do other things outside of looking after my daughters because, imagine, I already had three." And another reported, "Before [1980], it was survival. It was looking for food."

Despite these multiple reasons for isolation, however, women soon sought out the company of others to obtain information, alleviate their fear and make sense of their experience. A woman imprisoned and then exiled in the first year of the dictatorship shared this perspective:

> The people looked for the ability to organize, not only out of need in that moment but also having the need for news, to know things. Because it happened that all the information was controlled. So nobody knew what was happening because it was all official through the radios, the television, everything. Therefore, the things that everyone wanted to know couldn't be known through the collective communication that there was but through the information that moved in clandestine and underground [ways]... So, the people needed not only to organize themselves for events but also

to acquire information. And the other thing is that, psychologically, there also exists the need to be together to lose the fear. I mean when you are alone, you feel more fear than if you are in a group.

Students, who "had less to lose" and who had "lost fear," started to organize soon after the coup. A former student explained that as early as 1975, university students (and then high school students in 1976) began distributing political pamphlets against the regime. "Maybe they were very small things," she said, "but we felt solidarity in the work ... and there was more strength." Another woman recalled the repercussions of this early activism: "Before [1983] there had also been detentions of a lot of young people at the university that went out to the street... and many youth died in the street."

Around 1978, the Communist Party in Arica began to rearticulate. One Party leader recalled that the environment "began, not to soften, but to show more possibilities of organizing... I began to contact people from the [Communist] Party... in 1978 more or less, to make contact, because *los viejos* [male Party elders], made contact with me and I started to become politically active." This opened a space for many women who wanted to become active, even for those who had not previously participated in the Party. One woman explained:

> The truth is that I didn't get involved in the Communist Party because of conviction and doctrine. I didn't get involved because I loved the Communist Party nor because its ideology fascinated me much. I got involved in the Communist Party because it was the only party of the left that remained standing in Arica. Because MIR [Movement of the Revolutionary Left] was destroyed [and] the Socialist Party had completely disappeared. The Communist Party was quiet for about three, four, five years, you know, with the people disarticulated and without political activity. And it was the first party that started to rearticulate here in Arica ... So I decided to get involved in the Communist Party because when it rearticulated here in Arica, they had a job here. They offered you the possibility of doing a clandestine job, with security rules ... that could be efficient. I mean, because a struggle against a tremendous colossus like the dictatorship wasn't a joke, you know. So, I considered that the Communist Party gave you at least a minimum of security.

One woman said, "We were a Communist Party in clandestinity but we were big, big. We had many women." This launched a whole new life for many women, young and older, housewives, students and professionals — a life in a world where one must "learn to live in clandestinity... [because] that's how we worked, in a clandestine way, with pseudonyms, false names, false addresses." Despite the difficulties inherent in this way of working, women from political parties were very active at the community level. In Arica, political and social activity started to coalesce between 1980 and 1983. For example, politically oriented cultural activities, including theatre and musical groups, resumed during this time, AFAVIR (Association of Relatives of the Victims of Repression), "the first movement of women undertaken to publicly denounce [the regime]," was formed in 1981 and the *ollas comunes* (collective kitchens) surfaced the following year. In addition, from within the political sphere, groups of women began to form that would have a significant influence on the trajectory of the women's movement over the next few years.

One of these groups grew out of a Communist Party cell composed only of women. Discontented with the lack of education provided by the Party, one member of this cell unearthed contraband Marxist literature "to begin the political education part" on their own. For a year or so, from 1981 to 1982, these women, who eventually included some socialists and other women from the far left, studied whatever they could get their hands on, despite "information arriving in Arica a month after it happened."

Then sometime in 1983, a news article "fell into our hands," a half page that affected the women forever after. The article referenced a large gathering of Latin American feminists at a region-wide biannual conference held in Lima, Peru, earlier that year:

> We always got together and read about a topic, discussed a topic. And there appeared in the *Revista Análisis* a document that had to do with a feminist conference. And we read this and from there, we began to work from another angle. I mean, we began to question with this article and to discuss, and everything. That's how we began to discuss and we began to question that… inside the anti-dictatorship movement, the women are the ones that go to the front and, at the end, those that appear in the declarations are the men. And we began to talk from another perspective about the issue of women.

Like their sisters in Santiago, these women in Arica began to analyze state repression as the ultimate expression of patriarchal relations entrenched in the private sphere of Chilean society (Kirkwood 1986). They hoped to advance the anti-dictatorship struggle by incorporating a feminist analysis that would simultaneously contribute to women's advancement in Chilean society. These newly identified socialist-feminists "decided to transform that study group into an organization with the idea to bring along women from the Party and from other sectors."

In August of that same year, another group of women formed in reaction to the detention of four prominent Communist Party leaders. Their wives initiated the first public demonstrations against the dictatorship in Arica by occupying the courthouse to protest the detentions. One woman recalled:

> We took the courthouse and we fought with the judges, with everyone. We asked for an interview with the president of the court and then we took the court. We stood on the balconies with [many] police and all the people on the balconies. From there, we directed the people. As one [woman] would

lay down to rest, another would direct [the people]. We were there for two or three days and then they took us to prison. The police threw us from I don't know how high, and they pulled us out and took us to prison.

She goes on to explain the significance of this protest for the growth of the women's movement in Arica:

> From the roots of those four detentions, the women's struggle in Arica was born ... We were only four and from that moment was born the whole movement of social and political organizations. Because [before that] there wasn't anything, everything was clandestine. Then two people got together, then three people talking and then out of the air, we formed a group of ten. Ten people that faced the consequences and protested and, with the help of others, there started the women's struggle, everything started.

Thus, for one compelling reason or another, politically engaged women in Arica decided it was time to organize and expand their network. Of all that happened subsequently, one woman reflected: "Sometimes one [only] wants to walk a block but what happened for us in that block was a whole world." That "world" would now be public. However, to go public was dangerous. The women organizers well remember what happened the night they prepared the invitations for the meeting that was to inaugurate the movement:

> L. took all the letters that same night and at dawn the CNI [secret police] went to ransack her house and they took her husband to prison... So, L. had the letters. They arrived and she put them under the armchair in the living room ... [The commander said], "Sit down *señora*, don't be afraid." So, L. sat in the armchair underneath which were the letters because they were turning over all the cushions, all of them, and there were all the letters of invitation. Fortunately, the CNI did not discover them because L. sat on them. But the rest was all turned over.

Notes

1. The number of people killed at the school is contested. Depending on the source, the death toll is between 150 and 2000 (Equipo de Educación Popular n.d.; Rojas n.d.). In the text, I have used the statistic from Equipo de Educación Popular (n.d.).

2. Gabriel González Videla was the elected president of Chile from 1946 to 1952. A member of the Radical Party, his party came to power in a coalition that included the Communist Party. However, in 1948, he expelled communists from cabinet and then established legislation that made the Communist Party illegal, precipitating a period of persecution and imprisonment of communist leaders. For this brutal reversal, González Videla is known among the communists as "el Traidor" (the Traitor).

3. Salvador Allende was elected to congress in 1937 and was Minister of Health from 1939 to 1942. He was a senator for more than twenty years. He ran for president unsuccessfully in 1931, 1958 and 1964, and then again successfully in 1970 as part of

the Popular Unity coalition.

4.   According to Chavkin (1985), the JAP originated from a discussion between women's groups and the Minister of Economy. "The JAP was to operate in the neighborhoods. Women took an informal community census and set up a basis for rationing such items as sugar, rice, and bread. It was an unofficial operation, a kind of populist pressure action, to try to substitute for the anti-black market law that Allende tried and failed to push through Congress" (203). Fifteen hundred of these groups were established throughout Chile.

3

Act II — La Lucha
(The Struggle)

Genesis of the Women's Movement: October 29, 1983

On October 29, 1983 ... they lent us the centre for retired people and there
we met, about sixty women, militants of parties from the left. (Gaviola et
al. 1994: 161–62)

To an observer, a number of things would be apparent about the women coming to
this meeting: they are keen to act, they are already politicized and they have different
agendas. One of the feminist organizers explained that their purpose in bringing the
women together to integrate the anti-dictatorship and the feminist struggle was, in
large part, "to prepare women ... for what would happen after 'Pinocho' was out. That
was our proposal. That on par with working to get 'Pinocho' out, the women would
prepare themselves, study." Another feminist leader expanded on this idea:

> You had to be able to comprehend that these two things can go parallel,
> together. And also, it is necessary, isn't it, that you have to lay the founda-
> tion. That this is going to be for the long haul, and that we had to prepare
> ourselves. It wasn't just to go out in this moment, but it was from here
> forward. We had to know that a dictatorship was something very terrible,
> very grave, and that this was going to be for who knows how long. And that
> in some moment, we would have to take responsibility and that we had to
> make a sustainable thing that would permit you to form yourself as a person,
> socially, as we say, and confront things that were going to come later.

Having been warned that it would be difficult to persuade other women to this
perspective, the women prepared "a type of speech" the night before the meeting
to present their ideas.

However, the majority of women had come to the meeting with different intentions. They brought a petition denouncing the recent detentions and solicited
signatures from the women at the meeting. In the wake of disappearances and detentions, they perceived immediate and confrontational action to be the most urgent
need. For them, "study" or "preparation" as proposed by the organizers would have
to wait:

> In those times, there was a specific [need] of the moment that took away
> from the time to think about other things outside of that because today four

people disappeared and you, as a movement, have to go out to the street to struggle so that those four persons would reappear. So, that struggle that you had prepared for tomorrow, is no longer good for tomorrow because in the night there were five dead... In the night something worse had happened.

Moreover, as is often the case, Party comrades were suspicious, distrustful and misinformed about feminism.[1] According to some sources, the Communist Party "planted" women to actively oppose the feminist influence at the meeting. These women accused the feminists of being bourgeois, imperialists and traitors. Many women argued that the goals of feminism were neither consistent with nor as important or urgent as their commitment to bring down the dictatorship. "We thought that, in that moment, the work wasn't a gender struggle but that we had to, in some way, involve ourselves in creating a movement that would fight — in our own way or within our own possibilities — against the dictatorship." They imagined that they would democratically form an association of women that would organize such actions on a larger scale. But they felt manipulated by the organizers who "came with an executive already formed." Consequently, the organizers were faced with an "insurmountable wall" of opposition mostly from other members of the Communist Party. One woman described the clash of opinions that ensued:

> When we had to define, to make the Statutes, the letter of principles of the group, it came out that there was going to be a group of feminists, of the gender perspective and women's rights. And the fight began. [One group said] that there was a dictatorship and that we had to overthrow it first and we had to get together for this. Another group said that feminism [was important], that the woman had to re-establish her rights... First one and then another defended the feminist thesis. And then the other said that, no, first we will organize ourselves to protest the dictatorship and then when the dictatorship is gone, we will see to the other.

The outcome was to split the group into two women's organizations: Movimiento por los Derechos de la Mujer (MODEMU, Movement for Women's Rights) and Centro de Estudio de la Mujer (CEDEMU, Women's Study Centre): "There in that meeting, we stood up. We were fifty. Forty of us stood up and ten stayed. We left to form MODEMU and they formed CEDEMU."[2]

Powerful Women in a Powerful Movement: 1983–88

Without doubt, the meeting held on October 29 precipitated all the subsequent activities of the women's movement in Arica that were sustained in diverse forms until the end of the dictatorship. Was the role of women in the anti-dictatorship movement important?

Yes, undoubtedly. The statistics, the photos, the record — everything makes it clear that, in large part, the women of the country headed the whole protest, the whole movement. They were the first that organized, the first ones on the issue of the political prisoners, later the detained and disappeared. They were the ones that first went out into the street. In Arica also, we were the first ones that went out into the street as a protest. Getting organized, we women were the first. And many women. So many that we didn't even believe it ourselves when we saw them in the rally. It was impressive.

"Ask yourself," challenged one woman, "'who did [all the activities]?' The women, of course!" In Arica, the women orchestrated countless initiatives and events. In addition to their work within and across the two women's organizations, many of these same women simultaneously participated in other social and political activities in Arica. While women did not comprise the entire membership of these other elements of the anti-dictatorship movement, women activists outnumbered their male counterparts and were powerful influences during those years. For these reasons, I include a diversity of activities under the broad umbrella of the women's movement. In the following sections, I describe the work initiated specifically by the women's organizations, followed by examples of clandestine activities, acts of solidarity and resistance, and communal survival-oriented activities. Finally, I relate the work of human rights groups, political parties and movements and initiatives of the Catholic Church.

Women's Organizations

The two women's organizations, MODEMU and CEDEMU, overtly represented the women's movement in Arica. Despite their divergent philosophical stances on feminism and on the goals of the women's movement in Arica, there is no question that the women of both groups were united in one common objective — the downfall of the dictatorship.

Officially inaugurated on January 14, 1984, MODEMU was the larger of the two groups. Formed in reaction to the brutality of detentions and the exigency of disappearances, the women "worked to confront the dictatorship." "We wanted women in the struggle, women in the street confronting, fighting, setting up. That's what we wanted, women to shock them." As a result, "we had to dedicate ourselves to going out into the street every day. I mean *every* day in the street."

> So, we went out, we got together. We weren't fifty or sixty; we were 300, 400 women. We were women from the church, women from the parties, women from the social organizations, neighbours. Singly and clandestinely, we invited them. And they came and came and we went out.

Although their name suggests that they were concerned about women's rights (*derechos de la mujer*), and indeed an important women's right of that time was the right "to participate in the struggle," according to the members, MODEMU was never a feminist organization nor were its objectives feminist. The organization's name was a pseudonym, a common practice of the time to mask the identities of participants and the real motives of organizations for their own protection. As one leader admitted, "Anyone could believe that the purpose of our organization would be centred on the theme of gender, but it wasn't like that." Another explained the differences between MODEMU and the more feminist-oriented CEDEMU:

> We [MODEMU] fought in a direct way against the system, against the dictatorship. But [CEDEMU] made a struggle purely about women, in another form but where they valorized and wanted to improve the valorization of the person as a woman, as a gender. We did not work in that area.

CEDEMU was the manifestation of a distinctly feminist movement in Arica. The history of CEDEMU parallels the community-based feminist work documented in Santiago (see, for example, Valdés and Weinstein 1993). This small group of women worked in the *poblaciones*, raising awareness of the issues of violence and discrimination against women, while at the same time acting in concert with MODEMU and their political party comrades in other anti-dictatorship activities. From her personal experience, a CEDEMU participant highlighted CEDEMU's feminist work: building self-esteem and independence, supporting women in need, and critically integrating their work within the anti-dictatorship struggle.

> One learned to value oneself more, to love oneself more, to move away a bit from the yoke of the house. And apart from this, we did community actions, very nice social actions. We also helped many abused women, pregnant teens… in various sectors, in whatever sector where the presence of women was required. Sometimes we also went to visit the women that were [in jail] because they had small children, and [we went] to the hospital as well… Well, apart from this we also always went downtown to throw pamphlets, we met outside the cathedral to do a minute of silence, to sing the national anthem, to do all those acts against [the regime], to accompany the detained and disappeared… We were always, more than anything, fighting against the dictatorship.

From the beginning, CEDEMU was tenuously connected with the broader feminist movement in Chile through its relationship with MEMCH83. MEMCH was originally founded in Santiago in 1935 as Movimiento Pro-emancipación de las Mujeres de Chile (Movement for the Emancipation of Women in Chile). After eighteen years working for women's rights, especially for the right to vote (fully granted in 1949), MEMCH dissolved and resurfaced in 1983 as a network of forty women's organizations fighting against the dictatorship across Chile.

On numerous occasions, MODEMU and CEDEMU united and their activities merged together, making it difficult to distinguish between the organizations. As one leader recounted: "Eventually, these two options got together in the street and in the coordination to organize ourselves" (Gaviola et al. 1994: 162). The year 1984 was especially rich with creative collaborations. The first massive women's event that the two groups coordinated was held in the athletic stadium on March 8, 1984, for International Women's Day. Organized by MODEMU in collaboration with other organizations including CEDEMU, this event drew about 1500 people. According to a CEDEMU leader:

8 MARZO 1984
ARICA-CHILE

DIA INTERNACIONAL
DE LA MUJER

Pamphlet for International Women's Day, March 8, 1984, "Women for Life"

We succeeded in making a ceremony that made history in Arica. It was a cultural ceremony where we presented all the issues, with stage design, lighting, music and everything… It raised our spirits. I don't remember any manifestation against the dictatorship, right up to today, of the magnitude of that March 8th event. (Gaviola et al. 1994: 162)

Another organizer relished this triumphant example of their early efforts.

We hit 'em where it hurts on March 8th because we reached a huge goal — we made March 8th political, anti-dictatorial. We said what we wanted. And with permission! I think that the old guy [Pinochet] must have died to be thinking how, in what moment, they gave these women permission to do that.

While the stadium event is proudly remembered, the most memorable, poignant and lasting representation of the women's work together is Mujeres de Luto (Women in Mourning). One woman recalled the inception of the idea and described the inaugural event in which some 150 women participated.

First Mujeres de Luto, September 11, 1984, "Democracy"

That was an idea that, I remember, [arose] in a conversation with [another woman]. We didn't know what to do for September 11. So, we began to talk. What should we do for September 11? What to do? What to do? And suddenly we thought to get dressed in black... Now, how to do it? Well, there was the idea of getting the women together and, in the end, we decided to be at the cathedral for one hour in silence, dressed in black. It was right at the height of the dictatorship and here in Arica the repression was strong. So, it was hard. And on top of that, we had to do it in secret so that it wouldn't get out. It took a lot to convince the people because there was fear; I mean there was fear for sure. But, in the end, we accomplished it. And the strategic part of how we did it? Well, I worked in the church — I always worked in the church — so we got a sacristan of the cathedral who left the cathedral open for us, one door on the side. So we arrived. We all went as usual, not dressed in black, but dressed ordinary. And inside the church, we changed our clothes... At precisely twelve o'clock, we went outside and we were there for one hour. The police arrived with their helmets, with their shields, submachine guns, everything. But they were taken aback because of what we were going to do. And all our relatives were in the plaza and I believe that it was super emotional. When it finished, when the clock struck one o'clock in the afternoon... we sang the national anthem and everyone cried. [We had a floral wreath that said] "Democracy."

Another woman explained what happened next. "We were surrounded, all the women were very afraid because we didn't know what was going to happen when we left the cathedral... At the end, when we dispersed, everyone ran to the side because of the fear we had." During the years of the dictatorship, the event gathered greater numbers each year to a maximum of 600 one year.

Also in 1984, the two women's organizations attempted to work across political party lines with a new women's organization, Mujeres por la Democracia (Women for Democracy). The leaders wanted to distance the new organization from both the feminist label and the leftist political party affiliations in order to generate more participation from a broader spectrum of women. One woman explained that, at that time:

There wasn't a more pluralist organization that joined [together]... the blocs of opposition to Pinochet... Mujeres por la Democracia emerged because there was a vast movement of women who wanted to participate. First, those that weren't from a party, so they weren't going to go to organizations with a marked [political] tendency that already existed. Second, there were women of the church, many of them. Another reason was that there were some Christian Democratic militants, professional women [and] people that didn't have a party clearly defined. I mean, it was a way to open the spectre of participation... because we understood that not everyone was reduced to the four walls of a party but we had to incorporate more people. We had to add people.

For about three years, women from different sectors and organizations carried out diverse activities that included workshops on women's sexuality, basic household maintenance (e.g., plumbing, electricity), haircutting and civic education into which were inserted political and feminist content. However, this organization folded when women "returned to their political parties," no longer willing to put aside party differences.

Meanwhile, MODEMU and CEDEMU continued to organize many activities as the need arose and a routine emerged around key dates, such as March 8 (International Women's Day), May 1 (Labour Day) and September 11 (anniversary of the coup), requiring the coordination of "a calendar of protest activities." These were planned and scheduled public activities that were used to raise consciousness among the citizens and to articulate their opposition to the dictatorship. Manifestations, demonstrations, concentrations, protests, marches — all with particular nuances of meaning — occurred regularly with hundreds of participants. MODEMU's leadership had an "incredible power" of bringing women together, boasting one demonstration with 3000 participants.

Clandestine Activities

While many activities were public, others were clandestine, requiring high levels of secrecy for security. "To be able to do our clandestine work, we did it in the middle of the night so that no one would see us and we were all vigilant." Parents and children, husbands and wives, siblings purposely did not tell each other about their political involvement. Mothers knew the risk they took when they went to the streets and they suffered for the risks their children took. "In the end, we all took a risk that something could happen to you, that they could kill you, that they could detain you. And who's going to know if they assume that you are sleeping in your house?"

Clandestine activities that were intended to disrupt the regime included producing mimeographed oppositional material, making molotovs (small homemade bombs) or *miguelitos* (large nails twisted to puncture tires in the street) and spray painting. These were all potentially dangerous tasks, usually conducted after curfew with contraband materials, but most of the women did them anyway. One woman, a teacher and mother of teenagers at the time, carefully detailed these tasks.

> We studied how to make homemade mimeographs. We met in a rotation in the homes of some *compañeras* that were less risky and we prepared material [political pamphlets], what we called "*las palomas*" [the doves], making a call to citizen consciousness. Also, disseminating [information] when there were going to be some specific activities. In the house of a *compañera*, they made *miguelitos*. So, someone bought nails, a quarter [kilo] of nails, I mean, we put together various quarters of nails. At different times, we brought them to this house so that there they made the *miguelitos*. And in the night, someone went to get them and do the distribution… We did spray painting in the night. In the same way, we bought spray paint and we went out, those that lived in the sectors, and we went out with two or three *compañeras* to spray paint, making the paintings that corresponded to the slogans of that time.

Another mother living in one of the most combative *poblaciones*, with three sons who were heavily involved in the underground resistance and three younger children in los Pioneros (a Communist Party children's group), evocatively described her role in the "struggle in clandestinity" at the neighbourhood level:

> I didn't go out into the street much to protest because my preoccupation, my struggle, as we say, was more than anything in my home, because I lent my home for many clandestine meetings. There were high-level persons against the regime having meetings, showing us slides… and showing us films that they brought from Santiago… Also I lent my home for making *miguelitos* [and] those molotovs… There they had… the mimeograph machines; my sons were always making pamphlets… I was the whole day in my house dispatching things to the people. "We came to look for this. We came to look for this other." "Come in. Come in." And me watching and watching that nobody saw us. Looking for material, looking even for tires. "We're going to make barricades, we need wood, we need all this." And me [saying], "Sure, take it, take it.".… There were many things that I suffered in that time, like I say, without being an active militant or whatever. But that was my struggle. That was my struggle.

Acts of Solidarity and Resistance

Acts of solidarity and collective resistance were abundant in Arica; sometimes, entire neighbourhoods were involved in the struggle. As one *pobladora* said of her *población*, "there were very few who didn't participate."

Some measures were organized to provide emotional and practical support:

> There was a solidarity campaign that we did with the *compañeros* that were detained at that time. They were five *compañeras* [whose husbands] were detained in the jail in Arica, *compañeras* that participated in MODEMU. Some were leaders. And [we provided] help for them to be able to maintain themselves as well. For example, we tried to sell used clothes among our friends to put together some money to buy some food to make family [food] baskets for them.

One single mother with six young children warmly recounted her experience with "the famous Pascuas Populares [Popular Christmas activities]... [that were done] exclusively within the Communist Party":

> I remember one Christmas that was so emotional. I was with all my little kids, so hungry. And one night, knocking on the door, a disguised young person appeared and he gave me a package and he left. I never knew who he was but I knew that he was a kid from the collective in which I participated. Christmas bread, a chicken, jars of peaches and underneath, another bag with homemade games, old toys repaired by their hands. It was such a beautiful thing for sure because at that moment I didn't have anything to give to my children. [The youth] were running all over Arica where they knew that there were mothers alone, that their husbands were in prison or weren't there, or whatever, and they went there.

One task, often borne by women, was to "make a presence," to "bear witness" or to "make a denunciation." Sometimes mothers and neighbours watched out for youth during street actions and on the barricades. One mother got involved in the movement, in part, to alleviate the anguish she experienced when her children went out. "I went out to see where the youth were, what they were doing, for example. So they would realize that there were always people [watching out for them]." From her daughter's perspective:

> We were there putting together a barricade and all that stuff. And I suddenly looked to the front and there were a whole lot of older people in one entire corner. My mother told me that... there were many relatives of the kids who were there, of the youths that were there. So then when the military came, they started to yell, "run, run" because they knew that they were coming towards us. In the end, the people closest to you, or the neighbour that was involved in the Young Communists or the Party, had that role.

Pascua Popular during 1980s, "For Justice and Peace"

In an attempt to undercut the secrecy of detentions, neighbours were trained to shout out and make any kind of commotion or they left a public notice. "You made a [denunciation] when they took someone to prison," clarified one woman, "so that [everyone] would see that." She provided the example of a poster with the following message: "From this house, they took C. and his son. The CNI [secret police] has them." In another example, an entire neighbourhood responded instantly to word that all five members of a family had been detained. Neighbours bore witness to their forcible removal from the home, stood vigil at the family home and organized denunciations. The family members were released one by one over a number of months.

In one kind of demonstration (*los cacerolazos*), women went to the streets banging their cooking pots. Previously, middle- and upper-class women banged their pots to protest the Allende government in the time of contrived food shortages. During the dictatorship, poor women banged their pots to protest their growing poverty. In this example, a young activist convinces her mother to participate:

> I remember that I talked with my mother. I told her that they were planning a *cacerolazo*. They cut the lights in the streets and everyone went to the street to bang the pots and pans. But she didn't get involved in many things. She was afraid, she was very afraid. So I said to her, "*Mamá*, for how long are we going to put up with this?"... So, my mother cut the lights and suddenly, inside the house, I heard an uproar of pots and it was my mother that had gone to the street with a vengeance and she starts to call the neighbour women and she says, "bang the pots for the children, for everyone."... Obviously, the pot had to be thrown away, and another day there was no ladle in the house because it was broken. But it was worth it.

Some activities were creatively calculated to make specific political statements such as one designed to underscore the dire economic situation. "We went to the supermarket, the only supermarket that there was. Then, we filled the carts with groceries. And when it came to the moment to move to the cashier, we left them there." When they walked away from the unpaid groceries the women declared: "I can't take these because I don't have any money. My husband is unemployed. This is what I must buy but I can't buy it because I have no money." As one woman stated, "It was like leaving evidence of the things that were happening at the time."

On another occasion, fifteen to twenty women drew attention to social class divisions and the injustice of the military regime when they disrupted a special mass in the Catholic cathedral:

> The other thing we did… and [now] we think it was quite risky. Here in Chile, for September 18 [Chilean Independence Day], they do a *Te Deum*. It's a special mass that is celebrated in the cathedral in all the cities in the country, where all the authorities of the province attend and of course, the military and the armed forces, those with high rank. So, it's a day of ceremony where not even the community of that church participates but it is a special ceremony… [We decided to go there and mix in as best we could until] we would sing the national anthem. But only to where it was *our* anthem, without singing the stanzas that they added during the dictatorship, and add on a little yelling in the part that said "freedom" or "against oppression"… The anthem started and then we started our show. Of course, when they heard our voices, they began to turn around. Everyone was surprised, but they couldn't do anything, they were officiating the mass and they couldn't do anything. But in that moment that we did it, we were surrounded by military… I feel that it was like completing a commitment. It was something that we had to do and besides, it mutually fortified us.

One young university student, nine months pregnant, defiantly chained herself to the bars on the windows of the cathedral,

> as a form of protest against the accusations against the student leader, her husband, who is placed incommunicado in the Detention Centre… Her purpose was to remain there until they lift the communication ban and retract the accusations against [him] and moreover, she requested that a doctor attend the detained person. Police arrived on the scene and proceeded to tear the posters and to cut the chains with a special tool. Before this, they ordered the students and others to depart. (Se Encadenó Esposa de Dirigente Preso 1988: 7)

Because of her bold protest, in conjunction with a hunger strike conducted by a small group of students, the authorities admitted that they held her husband in custody

Folkloric group Chuccuruma performing in 1986, "In Unity the People Construct Democracy"

and moved him from the Detention Centre to a proper jail, where he remained incarcerated for two years.

Cultural forms of resistance and solidarity were equally important instruments in the anti-dictatorship struggle. As one woman declared: "The generation of the eighties was after all, a struggle to denounce, to go out practically every day to the street to do cultural acts." For example, the folkloric group, Chuccuruma, made an important contribution. Through music, dance, theatre and poetry, this group of young activists publicly denounced the dictatorship by defiantly singing the banned songs and reciting the forbidden poems — cultural symbols that condemned injustice and oppression, bolstered solidarity and offered hope. *Talleres populares* (children's events) effectively served the same purposes "with games [and] everything that would entertain the children. And between the puppets and the theatre, we denounced."

Some young women were part of the communist brigade of artists who painted murals and slogans in public places at night, only to have them whitewashed the next day by the military and then undaunted, to recreate their murals anew the next night. One such artist, while running away from the police on one particularly dangerous night, dropped her paintbrush and went back for it despite the danger — a testament to the vital significance of the role of art in the struggle and to the relentless courage of the artist.

Communal Survival-oriented Activities
Communal survival-oriented activities were plentiful across the country (and indeed throughout Latin America). Such activities were instigated in response to the women's difficulty, during the economic repression of the regime, in fulfilling their traditional roles as caregivers. Moreover, they fulfilled a powerful public and personal consciousness-raising function. In Arica, there were various kinds of

communal feeding activities. For example, in church courtyards, Catholic women cooked and served daily meals for university students in collective "dining rooms" (*comedores universitarios*).

Ollas comunes (collective kitchens) are probably the most well known of these types of activities and have been emulated in other regions of the world. Two neighbourhood leaders described the origin, purpose and functioning of the *olla común* in their *población*, the first and the largest in Arica with 120 families at one point. For one, a single mother of four, economic necessity was paramount but the other emphasized the consciousness-raising aspect. "More than anything, it was like a protest against the government because we had to do something to bring attention to the whole world." But it wasn't easy to get started. The women went house-to-house looking for people who could contribute and participate. People were afraid at first. The word "*olla*" (pot) was synonymous with "communist" and they had heard of the repression against the *ollas comunes* in Santiago. But, after a short period of operating secretly,

> We lost our fear. One day, we cooked with the military and shared the food with the tanks over here. Yes, later the door was open … At least, we were never detected; I mean they knew that there was an *olla* here because we had a military [person] on the corner and a policeman over there. It was because they were neighbours. It was never so hard as in Santiago, where the repression was worse.

The problem of cooking in huge quantities required a creative solution:

> We had to use washing machines, those big round washing machines. We sent them to be soldered below and we filled them to the top. There were hundreds of plates [of food] that came out of there because every family had four plates, five plates, ten plates.

The *olla común* was highly organized with an established schedule of roles, responsibilities and activities for buying, preparing and cooking the food as well as for organizational meetings, financial accounting and for selling favourite local foods to raise money to "buy more meat, for example." Politically, the organizers were from parties of the left but members included Christian Democrats and right-wing people. For this reason, the women "did not touch on the political theme" because, if they had, "most of the people would run away" or "immediately close their doors."

Human Rights Groups

As with the *ollas comunes*, human rights groups motivated by mothers' concerns for their loved ones were an integral part of the Latin American women's movement. In Arica, there were various organizations with this purpose, including AFAVIR (Association of Relatives of the Victims of Repression) and the Human Rights Commission, as well as underground human rights organizing. One of the most

Banner of the Human Rights Commission in a 1988 demonstration, "Human Rights"

demoralizing actions of the military regime in Arica was the detention of nineteen professionals in 1984, including the entire Human Rights Commission, leaving all of the other activists in Arica without the protection of human rights workers or legal representation. This tragic event is sadly remembered as la Pascua Negra (the Black Christmas).

A powerful human rights group was El Movimiento Contra la Tortura Sebastián Acevedo (The Sebastián Acevedo Movement Against Torture), named in honour of a man who, in 1983, burned himself at the steps of a cathedral in Concepción (the largest city in the south of Chile) protesting the detention of his son and daughter. In response to this tragedy, two months later, a Catholic priest created this non-violent human rights group. The group existed elsewhere in the country but, in the north, was most prominent in Arica. Members, both men and women, took a public, brave and non-violent approach to denouncing the abuses of the dictatorship. One of the group members described an action.

> We agreed to meet in a particular place that had to be a place that had a crowd because the idea was to denounce. Therefore, everything was organized and internally, there was a coordinator. And this coordinator established all the roles that were going to be completed by each one. And we went and gave the signal — the signal could be that someone would hug or kiss — and in that moment, all of us were summoned from different sides, pretending that we didn't know each other. So, in the moment that they greeted each other, all of us that were there, grouped together. Those that had the banner opened the banner and [then we] made the denunciation. The action had various parts. We clapped first, then we read something, we

made litanies, and afterwards we sang the song *"Yo Te Nombro Libertad"* and [after five minutes] the group dissolved.

Their evocative theme song, "Yo Te Nombro Libertad" ("I Name You Freedom," from the poem by Paul Eluard, music by Gian Franco Pagliaro), begins as follows:

> For the encaged bird
> For the fish in the tank
> For my friend who is in prison
> because he said what he thinks
> For the uprooted flowers
> For the trampled grass
> For the pruned trees
> For the tortured bodies
> I name you freedom!
>
> For the clenched teeth
> For the restrained anger
> For the knot in the throat
> For the mouths that don't sing
> For the clandestine kiss
> For the censured verse
> For the exiled youth
> For the prohibited names
> I name you Freedom!
>
> Chorus
> I name you in the name of all.
> By your true name
> I name you and when it grows dark
> when no one sees me
> I write your name
> on the walls of my city
> I write your name
> on the walls of my city
> Your true name
> Your name and other names
> that I don't name, for fear.
> I name you Freedom!

Political Parties and Movements

Many women belonged to el Partido Comunista (the Communist Party) or la Jota (nickname for the Young Communists). Some had also been in los Pioneros (The Pioneers, a Communist Party children's group) as youngsters. They participated in clandestine cells in schools, workplaces, the university and in the *poblaciones*. At the university, communist students organized campus strikes and student demonstrations. Others were active in their *poblaciones*, setting up barricades, mobilizing their neighbours and establishing collective responses for economic survival. One woman referred pragmatically to her role in an armed communist paramilitary contingent: "There were other things that were more important than the protests, although we didn't leave them aside because they were important too. But there were things that are more audacious... because it was not just about throwing a rock at the military. It was a thing of security... of the city."

Banner of the Communist Party (among others) in 1988 Demonstration

Some women belonged to the Socialist Party, one to the Christian Democrats and a few others to Movimiento Izquierda Revolucionario (MIR, the Movement of the Revolutionary Left). Although all political parties were banned, women who were active in these other parties and political movements participated in ways similar to those described for the Communist Party members above.

The Roman Catholic Church

Churches in wealthier neighbourhoods and those that served the military were aligned with the conservative element of the Catholic Church in Chile and were powerfully connected to the dictatorship. However, many Catholic parishes throughout Latin America responded to the philosophical positioning of the Catholic Church

March led by Catholic Church Parroquia del Carmen in 1980s, "Oh, Lord, End the Power of Bad Men"

that was promoted by the Second Vatican Council and the Second Latin American Bishops' Conference in the 1960s and that subsequently heralded the outbreak of liberation theology throughout the region. Liberation theology is promulgated on the belief that the mission of the church is to align with the poor and oppressed and to work for their liberation. The Catholic Church in Arica, as elsewhere throughout Latin America, made a distinctive contribution to the women's and anti-dictatorship movements from this liberationist standpoint. One woman who was very active in the church attested:

> The church in Arica was fundamental in all the work of recovering democracy... The church played a fundamental role in terms of welcoming the people and of being the voice of those who had no voice, of taking risks with the people who were oppressed.

Some churches in Arica held special significance in this regard, in particular Iglesia de la Sagrada Familia, Parroquia del Carmen and Parroquia Santa Cruz. These churches, with priests and nuns sympathetic to the anti-dictatorship movement, played a pivotal role in the movement by feeding students, by providing a safe place for clandestine meetings and by offering sanctuary to the pursued and persecuted.

An especially important offshoot of the Catholic Church was (and still is) the NGO, Servicio Paz y Justicia (SERPAJ, Service for Peace and Justice) from within whose auspices the Sebastián Acevedo Movement Against Torture was established. A branch in Arica was founded in 1979. One of the founders in Arica reflected on its role:

> I believe that SERPAJ was like the authority that permitted many people to get together, many people. Because we did a series of discussion encoun-

ters, all in the church. They were a bit camouflaged but it permitted us to get together and converse about what was happening and how we could reorganize and reconstitute the social fabric... So, beginning from those encounters, people who had the motivation regarding human rights, who were waiting for the possibility to get together with others to discuss, started to get together.

Such educational activities within the church were important in publicly identifying and condemning the abuses of the dictatorship. One privileged woman attributed her "metamorphosis" near the end of the dictatorship to a seminar about human rights abuses in Chile that she attended at her church. Once she realized that the whole apparatus of the dictatorship had deceived her, she "opened her eyes" and started on a totally new life course of feminist work with women in the *poblaciones*. Another woman was part of the first aid brigade organized by her church that tended to the wounds of those injured in neighbourhood street actions.

Summary of Women's Movement Activities
To succinctly convey the depth and the breadth of the women's participation in *la Lucha*, I repeat here a summary scripted by the research team (Chovanec, Bravo and González 2002).

> Along with the struggle in the streets, we had to organize ourselves, to do something more. And we went around adding, one woman, another woman, and there quietly, another.
> Women who had never left their house started to be invited or simply to invite themselves. They shared the same problems, the same disquietudes, the disinformation or the distorted information that came officially, the uncertainty, the "not having," of having to make do a lot of times (maybe the majority of the time).
> We felt afraid, but we met just the same, in the parish, in a house, we talked, we gave ideas. We had to throw out the dictatorship. We began to control the fear. Then came permanent and clandestine meetings. The *ollas comunes* and the collective buying emerged. Some returned to the militancy of the political party, some had never left it. The organizations: commemorating March 8, MODEMU, CEDEMU, Mujeres de Luto, Mujeres por la Democracia, the Association of Relatives of the Victims of Repression, the Association of Relatives of the Political Prisoners, the Sebastián Acevedo Movement Against Torture, etcetera.
> Women everywhere! Women defending their rights, their lives, their families. The feminine struggle and the feminist struggle. Histories entwined for the common reality.
> Democracy in the country and in the home! (And in the political parties too!) We were sharing, learning, educating ourselves and growing.

In reflecting on their learning from all this activity, one woman declared: "What *didn't* I learn?" The richness of the learning intrinsic to this period is captured in countless phrases related to the women's growth and skill development, phrases such as "it served to awaken me" or "the street was our school." Clearly, the women learned numerous practical skills simply because "it was necessary to know things" such as how to operate a mimeograph machine, make molotov cocktails, avoid detention, speak publicly, organize massive events on a moment's notice and cook for the entire neighbourhood. Together the women taught and learned from one another what they needed to know in order to manage or overcome the challenging material conditions of their lives. Self-esteem, self-confidence, empowerment and leadership skills were strengthened in the course of their activism. Tangibly and irrevocably, these women became increasingly aware of "the capacity of women to do things."

Many, like the woman quoted next, said that if not for the dictatorship, they would be stuck in their homes still, slaves to their husbands and children. "I achieved much more as a person and I grew more. I grew as a woman more in that time. All of that thanks to the dictatorship. If not for the dictatorship I would always have been more delayed in that sense." Through the explicit or implicit influence of feminism, women also gained a new perspective on themselves as women in Chilean society and acted from that position in the years that followed. As a result of the feminist influence, a younger woman proclaimed, "you have the capacity of a larger analysis and you have more capacity to see."

Without doubt, what the women cherished most from this period was their *solidaridad* (solidarity). This sentiment generated the most palpable nostalgia.

> The solidarity, the ties that were created between all of us, a very strong sisterhood. The pain of the other, the help that each one could offer, not only material but also emotional. I believe that that was very important... And I tell you that I believe that despite the time, despite that many have lost that permanent connection... every time we meet, even if we haven't seen each other for five or six years, it's an outward happiness, a very wonderful feeling... with a lot of happiness and a lot of caring. I believe that those ties are so strong that time won't forget or diminish them.

Solidarity was related to security, life and death, sharing, "profound" friendships, managing fear, common purpose and "maximum union." A *pobladora* picks up on the last point. "When we want to do something united, we can do a lot. When we are disunited, we do nothing. With unity and the struggle and everything synchronized, we did many things."

While the list of "many things" is seemingly endless, these were accomplished by a relatively small percentage of the population. Among the women, as many as 3000 might congregate for a massive demonstration but regular members were probably around a hundred women, half of whom participated in this research, and only a handful of women were in the organizing group. Despite their relatively small numbers, the women managed to project an image of alarming statistical significance, mainly by appearing everywhere that protest or denunciation erupted and by working endlessly and tirelessly "like ants." This "being everywhere" came at great cost, however. Women with children and husbands at home had "triple work because the woman went out into the street and she had to arrive home to cook ... [and she] had to watch her children." Others fuelled by the energy, passion and fearlessness of youth fit activities into almost every hour of every day.

> We slept very little. What happened was this: I got up at 7:00 to go to work. I finished working at 1:00. I ate lunch and from there, until 3 or 4 in the morning, [I was] in all of this. For example, we went to SERPAJ from 3 to 5. After that, we went to Chuccuruma from 6 to 8. From there, we went to the Association [AFAVIR] from 8 to 10. From there, we went somewhere else from 10 to 12. After that, we went to the clandestine activities in the street in the night, from 12 or 1 in the morning until 3 or 4 in the morning, doing things. From there, to sleep for 2 or 3 hours, [then] to work again. We slept little. But one goes around being involved, being involved, without thinking of it like an agenda.

The Movement in Transition: 1988–90

Towards the end of the dictatorship years, after five or more years of exhausting struggle, social movements were pacified by a number of significant events. During his visit in April 1987, Pope John Paul II deeply disappointed Catholics and non-Catholics alike in the popular sector by not speaking out against the abuses of the regime.

> For me, my hopes started to change after the visit of the Pope ... Without letting go of the inclination to get Pinochet out ... it pacified the social movements, but incredibly so. Even more, there was a tremendous manipulation of the social movement with the coming of the Pope because the truthful people wanted to talk and in the end, they didn't let them talk ... And after the visit of the Pope, I saw a change, a total and absolute change in many people, in many people, in a lot of the discourse, a lot of the radio, a lot of the music. Everything changed from this incredible influence, incredible. The people fell asleep with the famous discourse that everything will come from heaven ... that love was stronger than continuing to fight.

Another pacifying factor was the formation, in 1987, of the Concertación por la Democracia, the coalition of centre-left political parties negotiating with the regime. The coalition excluded the more revolutionary factions such as the Communist Party. The effect of this exclusion in the negotiation process was particularly pronounced in Arica due to the powerful position of the Communist Party historically and during the anti-dictatorship struggle. Moreover, the plebiscite in October 1988 in which anti-dictatorship activists marginally succeeded in winning the vote against continued military rule contributed to a false sense of security and an erroneous feeling that the battle was won and the work finished.

A critical turning point for the younger women in Arica was the death of one of their *compañeros* at a political activity very near the end of the dictatorship. On New Year's Eve 1988, many of the young anti-dictatorship activists from various movements and political parties had gathered around a roadway underpass where they were painting a protest mural and a New Year message when the police arrived. What actually happened remains unclear. However, the outcome was the death of a young activist, Salvador Cautivo, and the arrest of numerous students. The younger women speculated that there had been a breakdown within their own security. Amidst rumours and speculation, Cautivo's tragic death effectively destroyed the political zeal of many of these young women and prompted a critical re-evaluation of their political participation. Echoing others, one young woman pronounced, "My political moment ended in 1989."

These events occurring close together in time prompted a spiral of movement decline that was fuelled by many other factors such as emotional and physical fatigue, fear that the tenuous coalition could topple, disillusionment with the process and goals of the coalition, lack of a sturdy ideological basis to the movement and the return of traditional political actors (political parties and unions). Both the women and the literature credit the successful overthrow of the dictatorship in 1989 to the steadfastness of their purpose, but also to the narrow strategizing, utilitarian coalitions and single-minded goal of ending the dictatorship (see, for example, Waylen 1993). Today, the women remain perpetually puzzled and saddened about the demise of their once strong women's movement. Over and over again, with heads sadly shaking, women muttered, "*se fueron para la casa*" — they went home.

Notes

1. The tensions between feminism and socialism/Marxism are well documented. See, for example, Chinchilla (1992), Hartsock (1983) and MacKinnon (1997).
2. Later it retained the acronym CEDEMU but was renamed Casa de Encuentro de la Mujer (Meeting Place for Women).

4

Act III — La Continuación
(The Continuation)

Women Return to their Homes

It is ironic that the women expanded their sphere of action and influence beyond their homes during the dictatorship — an arguably inhospitable period for women's organizing — only to retreat to their homes again upon the return of "democracy." "We fought better in the dictatorship. It's sort of paradoxical," said a MODEMU leader. Women in Arica were well aware of the countless gender-specific and other social problems yet to be tackled in Chile. "It isn't the kind of work that [you can say] 'now we overthrew the dictatorship, done, the tyrant is gone.'" "We knew that it wasn't going to be so easy to eradicate seventeen years, that we had to continue the struggle." Thus, the current situation in Chile is particularly baffling for the women. As one young woman asked aloud, "Why did the woman who left her home to fight, return to her home?"

Representative of the most common explanations, one leader of the women's movement in Arica provided the following five-part analysis, which warrants inclusion in its entirety for its thoroughness and thoughtfulness.

I believe that [the women] were the motor of the social movement in Chile and it's a pity that it has been lost. [Q: What happened?] It passed. I believe that there were various factors.

One, the return of the political parties that, through their party activities, restricted the parallel activities. I mean, democracy arrived and the women went to their parties and to their home, those that didn't have a party. So, the organizations didn't continue to function. I believe that many people thought that with democracy there would be no need for more organizations. That was a big mistake. I think that was one of the things.

And another that has been eroded, that stopped the movement, is the loss of hope, the anger, the impotence to see that so many things that they had thought they were going to see in democracy haven't been possible in any of the three governments of the Concertación. And even less are they going to be possible in a government of the right.

And the other factor is that the women, unfortunately in the history of the women's movement in Chile — and I don't know, the world, I daresay — in Chile for sure, it is sort of cyclical. There are the big events that move great numbers of women, in the time of the suffragettes, in the time of MEMCH, in the time of the dictatorship. In the time of the Popular Unity

51

[government], the women were the first that went out to protest against the government, the women from the right. And it has always been cyclical like this. According to the events, there is mobilization for a time. These, I believe, are the factors.

And another is the incapacity of our movement to recognize the women's movement, to maintain a homogenous movement or to have had a common line of thought, to learn to work through the diversity, respecting the differences — a thing that we don't know how to achieve even in the feminist movement, much less in the other movements. There are fewer things that unite. There are many political disagreements. The political parties, I believe, have done no favours for the popular and women's movements.

And another thing is the church. The churches have stopped being the centre that we knew, at least in the period of the dictatorship, the centre of meetings, the centre where the women met, the focus of work, the focus of solidarity work — they lost this as well. The doctrine of the church has changed the political discourse of the church a lot, from what it was before to what it is now. The conservative church in Chile has a large presence and that influences women enormously.

So, in that aspect, I believe that those are the reasons for which the women's movement has not emerged. It hasn't re-emerged despite the things that have happened and despite having been such a strong movement.

Although the speaker humbly apologizes that she has not studied the issue, her analysis is consistent with the common elements identified in the literature (see, for example, Alvarez 1990; Craske 1998; Franceschet 2001; Hellman 1992; Schild 1991; Schuurman 1993; Waylen 2000). Other women echoed her analysis of the role of political parties in the transition. Some women blamed the political parties because "it was they that demolished what could have been a great organization of women [through] the lack of vision, the lack of tolerance, the lack of recognition of some questions." The women thought that it was a "great political error" to assume that other social organizations were no longer necessary to the political process "because, imagine the country that we would have now if they had taken advantage" of the women's solidarity, collaboration, creativity and organizational skills. However, when the political process was reconstituted, little space was left for the women's movement.

As *solidaridad* is the hallmark emotion of the anti-dictatorship struggle, so is *pena* the key emotion of the post-dictatorship era. *Pena* is a word with complex emotional significance that is not easily translated into English. For these women, *pena* signifies a deeply felt combination of bitter pain and sorrow arising out of severe disappointment at the outcome of their efforts. "It's good that we achieved democracy. I believe that the objective was completed, that is, if we no longer have the dictatorship. But, for me, I have been disillusioned by the democracy that we have." The word *pena* projects the image of the sad and frustrated shaking of one's head as one painfully contemplates a promising destiny that remains unfulfilled.

Nonetheless, many women also use the idiom "*vale la pena*" in the context of their movement participation. This expression means that they remain stalwart in their conviction that despite the limited outcome, their movement was worth every bit of pain and sorrow. The older women were especially unequivocal in this respect. "I don't regret anything that I did, nothing, nothing. If I had to live it again, I believe that I would live in the same way or maybe with more risk, try to do more things." But not all of the younger women were as certain. "Sometimes I think that if I were born again, I don't know if I would do it again."

Some women felt that they themselves did not adequately take advantage of the power at hand, that somehow they let opportunities slip through their fingers. As one young leader lamented, "We had so many women in our hands, so many; an incredible power of calling the women together." In recounting the first Mujeres de Luto, another woman tearfully interjects, "I get angry, you know, because we haven't taken advantage of all that."

Women also reflected on the educational elements that were missing in their activist experiences. One of the youngest women activists sagely pondered, "Maybe we lived as *pobladoras* and we didn't realize either what was necessary to maintain an organization, what was necessary to maintain an activity with others, I mean, more than just greeting each other." Often, women said that they were not prepared for what was to come, not adequately educated politically. An older woman reflected, "I believe that we lived responding to daily happenings, in the contingency, we lived the contingency. And afterwards, each one went to her home. What was missing was the preparing of ourselves for afterwards." The younger women complained that they were not prepared for democracy, having never experienced it themselves. Many women thought that citizens were missing the "elements for democracy." "The people today have no possibility to make their own decisions because they don't have the tools." "We women weren't prepared to be involved... there was no work to say how we were going to maintain democracy and maintain it in good form."

Chile's Pseudo-Democracy

Although some women were more cynical and disillusioned than others, none of the women were satisfied that they had achieved what they thought they were fighting for. This sentiment was common: "In truth, I was happy that 'Pinocho' was gone and I knew that difficult times were coming, but I never thought it would be so much. I thought that *something* would happen." Instead, the list of the women's disappointments about the current situation in Chile is long and remains unchanged despite four successive coalition governments.

- Regarding the human rights abuses: amnesty, immunity from prosecution, lack of accountability and no answers about the whereabouts of the disappeared.

Unlike in neighbouring Argentina, Chile has steadfastly refused to take firm action against the perpetrators of the abuses, encouraging instead a "turn the page" attitude.

- Continuation and escalation of the privatization of industry and public services such as health care, pensions, unemployment insurance, education and utilities. For example, in the guise of "health care reform," the government promoted Plan Auge, the neo-liberal vision of health care, in 2002. The women recognize that only the wealthy benefit from the privatization of social and health services.

- No reform to the constitution that was written and passed by the military government in 1980. "As long as there is no change in the constitution, we are going to continue as we are."

- The binominal electoral system that favours the right. Although the "winners" are determined by a complicated mathematical formula, most Chileans seem to understand it clearly and recognize the built-in discrimination against the far left.

- Ongoing poverty. One unemployed older woman, who had raised six children mostly on her own while an underground leader, equated her grinding poverty to violence. "Is it not violence to be living every day thinking about what I will cook tomorrow, where I will work, where I will live? This is violence. And everyday we are violated, women above all because we are the leaders of the home, those that educate the children."

The women recognized that these issues are all related to neo-liberalism and are legacies of the dictatorship but, beyond that, they felt betrayed by the Concertación. The women especially blamed the socialists for their "political turnaround" and "broken promises." They criticized politicians for "accommodating" to the situation inherited from the previous regime and for "taking advantage" of political openings. Especially disparaged were those who came from exile to assume high posts in the new government and those who had "abandoned" the Communist Party to join the government in power. Additionally, people are very bitter about *pituto* — the pervasive practice of giving jobs only to members of the reigning political party. Women who were somehow connected to the government in power were the most critical of the current situation. Cracks in their allegiance to the party in power were visible. They understood the need for caution in the early years of the transition but were later frustrated at the perpetually "slow" response to social problems and became discouraged when "you see that there are no changes." One younger woman who was working for the government at the time of the interview was extremely disillusioned about the political system:

> And the great leaders in whom you trusted, you realize that today they all negotiate to have that tiny quota of power that they don't want to lose. So, what do I think of all that? That really we were foolish instruments that were prepared to lose our skin and that the truth is that these guys that

lead the whole democratic process today, the only thing that they wanted was… to take turns in office, nothing more.

Unbridled cynicism is apparent in the women's many terms for the current system in Chile (e.g., "pseudo-democracy," "so-called democracy," "democracy, in quotes," "supposed democracy," "the famous democracy") and in the derisive references likening the current situation to the previous dictatorship (e.g., "white dictatorship," "civil dictatorship," "dictatorship in suits and ties"). To the laughter of others, one woman said, "it is a penis that has only changed its underwear." Lingering beneath the joke, however, is a serious critique. In 2006, the women envisioned little change with the possibility of a woman president. One asserted, "She is not going to be sensitive to social and women's issues; I think, she's not interested." Another woman observed, "The way power works has not changed by having women in cabinet so far."

Referring to the shift to the political right evident in recent elections, one woman issued a general warning:

> That gives us some pretty interesting signals that we should reflect upon… It shows us where our country is strongly going at this time — to a government of the right, but a government with more terrible characteristics than has come before. Why? Precisely because of a hidden populism. Today, the right in Chile has the banners of the struggle that the left had, the same discourse. "We must change." "The poor have nothing." And this is all disguised, so it is very dangerous. And it is dangerous precisely because our country and our people are not going to realize when they have another dictatorship on top of them… a civil dictatorship. Not with uniforms, but with ties and whatnot, that, in the end, is the same because they move the same.

In all kinds of ways, other women concurred: "There is no democracy, because democracy is not a question of a title. Democracy is a question of effective participation of the people. And there is none. Because they closed all the channels to the people."

The Women's Movement in the New Millennium

What then became of the women's organizations in Arica? Remember that for the majority of the women, the outcome of the meeting in October 1983 was that "first we will organize ourselves to protest the dictatorship and then when the dictatorship is gone, then we will see to the other" ("the other" referring to feminist/gender issues).

Since the final days of the dictatorship, CEDEMU has remained an established but marginally funded NGO that tenaciously carries the torch of a much-diminished feminist movement, although other similar organizations have recently emerged.

CEDEMU event for International Women's Day, March 8, mid-1990s

A small team composed of elder and younger activists focuses on women's rights, needs and issues (e.g., reproductive rights and violence against women) through a weekly radio show on women's issues and project work in the *poblaciones*. Of the success of their work, a CEDEMU leader reflected:

> The women will never see things the same way again. I mean, they have the information that allows them to reflect and that allows them to analyze, and that allows them to question… And together with that, incorporating the issues of women, of gender and… the political consciousness they have. So this is a question that the women — at least the women that passed through CEDEMU, the women that heard our discourse, the women that came to know what we were saying and what we were doing — no longer can say that they don't have the elements to be able to reflect, to be able to analyze the issues.

MODEMU continues to exist marginally, mostly within the Communist Party. However, it still carries the power to call together women for specific events and tries yet "to reactivate the organizations… [so] that there would be civic education." Of the other parallel organizations that were mainly populated and led by women, SERPAJ is probably the most solidly established social organization in Arica at this time. As part of a national organization, it continues to work with the poorest families, many of which are headed by lone females and who experience multiple problems, including drug abuse. The *centros de madres* (mothers' centres) retain the more conservative character instilled during the dictatorship, and the *juntas de vecinos* (neighbourhood councils), while still having significant numbers of women in leadership positions, are shifting ideologically to the right. A handful of women anti-dictatorship activists were elected or appointed to government positions in Arica in recent years. These women try to listen and to respond to the concerns of citizens but they feel isolated with inadequate support to "do good work" in the community.

The official government apparatus for women, SERNAM, a concession won by the feminist contingent during coalition negotiations, holds little relevance for the women in Arica today. Indeed, few are even aware of its existence. A woman working in the government observed, "Women [in Arica] don't feel represented by SERNAM ... The policy of SERNAM has come from very high up; there is very little participation ... There has to be a re-evaluation of the policies of SERNAM." For those who participated actively in the women's movement and still work directly with women in the popular sectors, it is especially galling that SERNAM arose from their struggles but is no longer responsive to their needs. In the opinion of a CEDEMU leader, "The Concertación has lost the possibility to do many things with SERNAM because they could have mounted a fine women's movement from there, working with women for real change, but they blew it."

While many commentators critique SERNAM's policies and perspectives, especially its institutionalization and distance from the grassroots (Schild 1998, 2000; Waylen 1997, 2000), some predict a possible rearticulation of the women's movement in Chile as evidenced by the formation of networks that represent a collection of diverse women's organizations who are strategically using the discourse of women's equality offered by SERNAM to get their demands met (Franceschet 2003). Two emerging women's networks in Chile are Red de Mujeres de Organizaciones Sociales (REMOS) and ANAMURI (a network of indigenous and rural women).

There is, however, little evidence of such organizations in Arica. Many women admitted to "retreating" or "opting out," to being "inactive" or "stagnant" and most had "abandoned the [party] militancy." When asked directly in 2002, a CEDEMU leader said, "I don't see anything yet, unfortunately not. There have been attempts but nothing has prospered ... I don't see an emerging movement." A MODEMU leader expresses her aggravation at the retreat of women in the following words:

> There is nowhere to go to try to get the women out of that numbness. It's like a lethargy. It's like we are so full of problems, *so* full of problems, that one whines every day. But you see that they do nothing. I don't know if the television and the soap operas stunted the mind of those women activists.

Part way through the transition period, there was a general exodus from political parties among the women. Disillusioned with their party's inability to adapt to changing times, to attract youth and to deal with women's issues, some switched parties and many left altogether. One younger woman declared, "If I want to participate politically, I don't need to belong to a party." More recently, however, women have begun returning to formal party membership. Moreover, the women identified "spaces of participation" such as grassroots organizations of women and local NGOs

Mujeres de Luto, September 11, 2007

working with youth or indigenous peoples. There are many women in leadership positions in the *juntas de vecinos*, NGOs, municipal and provincial governments and in student councils. From CEDEMU's perspective, "the little influence that the women's movement has is through a small movement, and achievements [are made] because there are groups of very committed women that move things."

One of the most enduring representations of the women's movement in Arica is Mujeres de Luto. At this event held annually since 1984 on September 11, the anniversary of the coup, the women still stand on the steps of the cathedral dressed in black for one hour of silence to bring attention to the injustices of the dictatorship. Over the years, the women added other activities, such as a march to the cemetery. According to the women, this event endures "because it is a space of vindication from the point of view of human rights" and because it "is also a symbol of the strength of women." Some women say that "there is a commitment that can't die, that we still have to be there." Others have stopped attending, and a rupture in the leadership prompted one woman to initiate a solitary act across from the cathedral. Only one woman said, "I withdrew because the objective for which we were working was democracy and it was achieved." Today, the event carries on with fewer numbers, except for the notable exception of the thirtieth anniversary of the coup in 2003 when 200 women participated. In recent years, the event has attracted more young women who attend with their mothers and grandmothers (H. González, personal communication, September 11, 2006).

Although the women's optimism for renewed political engagement is tempered with caution, some women, especially the older women, hold fast to their conviction that the future is hopeful. "I have confidence that, in some way, things will fall from their own weight… There is a saying that hope is the last thing lost." A few of the older women described themselves as "dreamers," "believers," and "optimists," and there is some hope among the women that the youth will "make a better society." As one woman concluded:

> I am going to continue to struggle because I believe that it is the only way that human beings can go forward — continue to dream, to believe in a utopia and to have internal strength. Because I believe that what I think is just, it is correct, it is what we have to do. Suddenly, we find ourselves with difficulties, with problems, but we are going to go forward… I believe that women will again show the way.

A New Generation of Activists

Indeed, there are new and optimistic signs that suggest that the women's movement in Arica may be dormant but is by no means dead. The women's dreams and hopes for the next generation might yet be realized in a new generation of activists, many of whom are young women.

On April 24, 2006, Chilean high school students initiated the first of a series of demonstrations, strikes and school takeovers demanding that the government ensure equal access to a quality education for all (Vogler 2006). The student movement, dubbed the Penguin Revolution because of the colour of the students' school uniforms, was organized by the Coordinating Assembly of High School Students (ACES), a group formed through the merger of political youth organizations. At a national strike on May 30, 2006, demonstrating secondary students, along with many university students, totalled between 600,000 to one million (Internationalist Striker 2006, para 22) and effectively immobilized almost all of Chile's schools and universities (Vogler 2006). Protests continued in various forms throughout the 2006 school year, and then, disgruntled with the slow pace of action on their issues and unsatisfied with the proposed changes to education legislation, the students resumed their protests in each of the succeeding school years (2007 and 2008).

The students lobbied for free bus fare, waiving the university admissions test fee, reform to the full-time schoolday policy and, most importantly, abolition of the law to privatize the education system. For the students, the LOCE, the *Ley Orgánica Constitucional de Eseñanza* (*Organic Constitutional Education Law*) — introduced just one day before Pinochet surrendered power in March 1990 — is a distressing example of the neo-liberal legacy left by the dictatorship. Under the LOCE, "the state drastically reduced its role in the educational sector" and based the new system on "free markets, private management and profit-oriented education" (Alarcón Ferrari 2007: 6). In formidable opposition to the LOCE, the Penguin Revolution grew rapidly into a national movement protesting the neo-liberalization of education in Chile and eventually aligning with broad-based movements challenging neo-liberalism across all sectors (e.g., education, pensions, housing). (See Chovanec and Benitez 2008 for

Students protest outside the cathedral, June 6, 2006.

a discussion of the LOCE and the Penguin Revolution.) Following the lead of the classmates in Santiago, students in Arica recognized the need to struggle for equal access to education. In the words of one of the woman student leaders in Arica:

> I believe that more than anything, the movement [started] because we youth that were gaining consciousness, in time we began to realize that [our] education wasn't very good and that there weren't the conditions for it to be good. The movement began in Santiago and then we followed them. We started the movement here because we realized that there wasn't equity, that not everyone had access to the same kind of education. Because of the capitalist system that we have, certain sectors of education are private and others are municipal. So, obviously in the private part, they pay more to be in that kind of school and there they get a good education. The municipal schools have a lot to do with the mayor; the money that they receive is not well distributed among the schools so it happens that those schools and the kind of education [in those schools] are terrible. Therefore, there

is inequality and, in the secondary school movement in Arica, we find this unjust. Why, if we are all students, do we have to get a different kind of education and some have to get better than others? More than anything, this was what started this struggle.

The student movement came as a surprise to many because of the marked decline in political mobilization in the aftermath of the dictatorship. Not since the massive mobilizations in 1983 to 1989 has there been an uprising of this magnitude in Chile; nor has there been, during almost two decades of the elected government of the centre-left coalition, any direct assault on the legacy or the legitimacy of the neo-liberal socio-economic order left in the wake of the dictatorship. In the opinion of the Penguins leader quoted above, "I think that the people that were fighting [during the dictatorship] are not present [in the struggle] now because they are afraid that something could happen again."

Yet, the Penguins have stormed onto the political stage in Chile, demanding (and getting) audiences with the president, causing ministers of education to be fired and prompting President Bachelet to move on new legislation to replace the LOCE, the *Ley General de Educación,* which she initiated on April 6, 2007. As predicted by Vogler (2006), "the student movement placed education at the top of the political agenda and paved the way for reform of the ... LOCE" (para 20). However, critics complain that these reforms fail to address the disastrous fallout from the LOCE, particularly ι now entrenched system of inequality based on socio-economic means. Like the vomen activists who preceded her, one young activist in Arica recognizes the need r a long-term commitment to the struggle. "Our proposal is for free and public ite education ... This year again we will continue with marches. We are going to ɔntinue with our proposal until the end ... until we succeed."

Through the ideologically informed mobilization of their grandmothers and ɛ bold activism of their mothers, women in the current generation of activists are ₐ scendants of the anti-dictatorship struggle. In the current generation of student ders, one glimpses the same sorts of family and political party influences and ₐ tivations as those experienced by their elders:

What happened is that I am the daughter of a worker and my mother is a housewife. Therefore, I realized that my father wasn't well paid and we had many needs. So, I began to look for a way to help in what was happening now. So, I entered the Communist Party. That has also helped me. And then I realized that one of the ways that I could help my family and many other families was through education. But first, I had to realize that the education is not very good, it isn't of good quality. So now I am fighting for a quality education that is equitable for everyone ... Both things have influenced me in the sense that in my family are many material needs. But also, the Party influenced me in the sense that I started there with a minimum of consciousness, but they showed me a little about the injustice and indignity of the world. So, they taught me a lot. And also, for my part, I have studied all that they taught me and I realized that there is often much inequality in the world and, because of this, you have to fight day by day and that, more than anything, there is a time for the struggle. And I am in that moment.

So, the movement re-emerges in a new moment. It continues in new forms with new actors as women across generations perpetually negotiate the "politics of despair and the politics of hope" that are the legacy of yesterday, the reality of today and that will define the future of the women's movement in Arica in the years to come.[1]

Notes

1. Adult education professor Michael Law suggested the idea of the "politics of despair and the politics of hope" in his closing remarks at the 2004 annual conference of the Canadian Association for the Study of Adult Education. For him, it represented a summation of the sentiments revealed in numerous paper presentations on social movements at the conference.

Part 2
Learning and Education
in Social Movements

Introduction

Since it is not possible to separate politics from education, a pedagogical act is political and the political is pedagogical. (Freire 2004: 115)

In Part 1, I attempted to portray the passion, the perseverance and the polarities of the women's movement in Arica, Chile. In Part 2, I engage with the literature and with theory to analyze the pedagogical dimension of the women's movement.

First, in Chapter 5, I describe the research study on learning in the women's movement in Arica including theory, context and method. In Chapters 6 to 8, I focus on three key analytical themes that relate to learning and education. In Chapter 6, I address the question, "How do we learn political consciousness?" I introduce a historical materialist understanding of the development of political consciousness, highlighting the importance of early learning and active engagement. The focus of Chapter 7 is the question, "What is social movement praxis?" Using the example of the problematic division of the women's movement in Arica into two women's organizations, I analyze the importance of praxis — the dialectical relationship of reflection and action as explicated by Marx and later translated to the field of adult education by Freire. This example demonstrates the importance of inserting a deliberate ideological element into movement activism that augments critical social analysis and provides a vision to guide the movement. Through an exploration of the learning and development of the younger participants of the movement in Chapter 8, I consider "How does participating in social movements change lives?" Combining the empirical data from this study with literature from other social movement studies, I look at the helpful and harmful consequences on the women's social/political and personal/interpersonal lives as well as the effect of emotions and trauma on social activists.

Finally, in Chapter 9, I state my conclusions about the role of the adult educator in social movements. Drawing on Antonio Gramsci's work on political education, I explicate the dialectical relationship between the organic role and the intentional role of adult educators in social movements and identify three "political-pedagogical" (Freire 2004) entry points — early learning, political parties and social movement continuity structures.

5

The Research Study

Theory must start with people's self-understanding, with giving an account of people as agents whose practices are shaped by their self-understanding.... This requires a close engagement with the agents — a mutual exchange between the "subjects" that are written about and the critics who write about them.... An interpretive approach grounded on how people understand themselves as creators and practitioners of their world is increasingly recognized as necessary. (Escobar 1992: 63)

Introduction

Social movements are sites of profound learning — sites where knowledge itself is contested and constructed, where identities and subjectivities (both individual and collective) are defined and redefined, where citizens are formed and where oppression is named. These activities, so integral to social movements, are clearly political learning processes. Any account of social movements and social activism demonstrates the central importance of this pedagogical dimension. Griff Foley's (1999) pedagogical "reading" of Sonia Alvarez's research on the Brazilian anti-dictatorship women's movement is one such example. Within the labour, feminist, peace, human rights, anti-globalization and environmental movements are numerous educational activities, from awareness-raising and skill-building workshops to the highly informal learning of action-reflection cycles. "Significant learning efforts are taking place within the many groups making up these movements... members select, critique, generate, organize and distribute knowledge" (Kastner 1993: 143). However,

> While systematic education does occur in some social movement sites and actions, learning in such situations is largely informal and often incidental — it is tacit, embedded in action and is often not recognised as learning. The learning is therefore often potential, or only half realized.... To more fully realize the value of such learning we need to expose it. (Foley 1999: 3)

The story that unfolds in these pages is part of research conducted for a doctoral thesis on learning in social movements (Chovanec 2004). In the remainder of this chapter, I briefly review the basic theories and rationale for the study of learning in social movements and describe the research approach used in the study upon which this book is based.

Social Movement Theories

How and why citizens collectively engage in social action has captured the attention of scholars for many decades. Adult education scholar John Holst (2002) chronicles two centuries of social movement theorizing in which "the dominant paradigm sees collective behavior as ultimately irrational" (29). However, the massive social mobilizations of students, women and civil rights activists in the 1960s prompted theorists to rethink social movements as an important element of political action, not as an activity outside of normal behaviour as was previously theorized. This led to a flurry of social movement theorizing from the 1970s to 1990s, which spawned two major schools of social movement theory: Resource Mobilization (RM) and New Social Movements (NSM). RM theory studies how social movements operate, looking particularly at resources, interests, strategies and political opportunities. NSM theories focus on why social movements arise. In contrast to old social movements such as the labour movement, theorists argue that new social movements are struggles to control the cultural sphere rather than the economic sphere and to defend the autonomy of civil society against the encroachment of the state and the economic sphere in a post-industrial society. (For a discussion of the differences, see, for example, Carroll 1997; Cohen 1985; Escobar and Alvarez 1992; Holst 2002). Many theorists suggest that the two theories can "inform each other" (Cohen 1985), allowing a for a hybrid approach that is more easily adapted to analyzing diverse socio-political contexts.

Since the 1990s, and particularly from within feminist theorizing, attention to issues of power, privilege and exclusion within and across movements as well as intersections of race, gender and class have challenged social movement activism and scholarship. New theorizing by scholars such as Mahrousse (2008) and Gouin (2009) use the work of anti-racist feminists Bannerji (1995), Mohanty (2003) and Razack (2007) to critically examine these issues.

In addition, newer theorists cite concerns about the growing gulf between activism and theorizing (see, for example, Bevington and Dixon 2005; Croteau, Hoynes and Ryan 2005; Frampton et al. 2006). During the 1960s and '70s, campuses around the world were sites of radical theorizing and action, and social movements were populated by intellectuals — both organic (arising from the movement) and traditional (academics). However, in the post-sixties era, which spawned a plethora of social movement theorizing, social movements increasingly became objects of study by outside observers (Frampton et al. 2006). Actual activism receded further into the background as academics who were no longer actively engaged in social movements and no longer informed by activist experience developed academic theory that was increasingly disconnected from the realities, experiences, concerns and needs of social movements. Social movement theories were formed and debated by academics in a self-perpetuating theoretical dialogue while activists carried on with the real work of trying to change the world, forming working theories when time and energy permitted. "The result is an artificial divide between the practice of social change and the study of such efforts.... Both activism and theory, we contend, are diminished by the failure to integrate the two" (Croteau et al. 2005: xiii).

Newer sociological approaches purport to reinvigorate the activist-scholar and to mutually engage both practice and theory and, therefore, to be more relevant to and within social movements. One is "political activist ethnography," an approach based on Dorothy Smith's institutional ethnography. According to Frampton et al. (2006), it is a "form of knowledge production designed explicitly for activism" (8) because the approach focuses on "an 'insider's' knowledge of ruling regimes based on the daily struggles and confrontations that social movements are already engaged in" (9). Another approach, drawing partly on cultural studies (e.g., Stuart Hall, "the politics of signification"), is called "collective action framing." Framing "focuses attention on the signifying work or meaning construction engaged in by social movement activists and participants and other parties" (Snow and Corrigall- Brown 2005: 222).

Both these approaches are of interest to an adult educator because they highlight processes of reflexivity, analysis, knowledge production, consciousness, epistemology and ontology. These are all pedagogical terms — they refer to learning and to education. According to activist ethnographers Frampton et al. (2006), pedagogy "is often used to talk about exploring how knowledge is produced. In order to investigate how ruling regimes operate, it is essential to be asking how we know" (34). Invoking a concept reminiscent of adult educators Horton and Freire (1990), they describe a process of extending activists' knowledge by starting from what they already know and making it more explicit. A.K. Thompson (2006) specifically cites Freire in his analysis of the "pedagogical moment" prompted by the occupation of the University of Guelph (Canada) president's office in 1997. Authors in Croteau, Hoynes and Ryan's (2005) edited book on collective action framing make repeated references to the learning and theoretical work done by scholar-activists. For example, Ryan (2005) "builds ongoing two-way learning relationships" between "social movement theorists and collective actors" (117).

In recognizing the vital importance of the pedagogical dimension of social movements, Thompson (2006) argues, "education, research, learning and struggle must each be emancipated from constraint and become aspects of the others" (101). Frampton et al. (2006) urge social movement scholars to "focus more attention on the pedagogy of activism and the teaching, learning and knowledge creation that takes place through activism" (267).

Adult Education and Social Movement Scholarship

It is upon adult educator-activist-scholars in partnership with other activist-scholars that this task must fall. The heritage of "adult education (or at least a substantial part of it) has always been associated with social change, social action, social movements, community development, and participatory democracy" (Spencer 1998: 62). However,

Much of the radical adult education that has taken place, largely informally, has occurred in meetings, protests, cultural events, and the day-to-day activities of social movements and organizations instigated by people who do not necessarily consciously consider the educational aspects of what they are doing. ... In other words, the field of adult education and the activists overlook much vital educational work for politics. (Holst 2002: 5)

Notwithstanding the frequent complaint that social movement academics and activists have paid little attention to learning, adult education scholars published some early theoretical work in the 1990s on learning in social movements (Dykstra and Law 1994; Finger 1989; Holford 1995; Kilgore 1999; Welton 1993). More recently within adult education, a concept dubbed "social movement learning" is capturing attention. In a series of publications, adult education scholar Budd Hall (Hall and Turay 2006; Hall 2006; Hall and Clover 2005) has begun to theorize the "Canadian tradition of social movement learning." Based on a review of the literature, his research team reports:

> Canada is a leading country for the study of adult education and social movements. The social movement learning tradition, which is at least one of the foundations of the contemporary adult education movement in Canada, continues to attract research and knowledge mobilization across both the university and community-based intellectual community. (Hall et al. 2006: 260)

Hall and Clover (2005) define social movement learning as both the informal learning of people involved within social movements as well as the learning that takes place in the broader community as a result of social movements and their actions. They assert that "reflection on the tacit skills being learned by social movement activists is of critical use in strengthening and extending the power and reach of social movements today" (587). Echoing the sociologists referenced in the previous section, Hall (2006) believes that "systematic investigation into the learning and knowledge strategies of social movements" would contribute to social movement scholarship across disciplines (236–37). In the 2006 Canadian *State of the Field Report on Social Movement Learning*, Hall and Turay (2006) identify a wealth of descriptive case study research on social movements throughout the world conducted by a number of Canadian and other adult education researchers. However, they argue that the construct of social movement learning is "underconceptualized" (12) and that there is little evidence of theory development. According to Hall et al. (2006):

> Many researchers note the importance [of] educational activities within social movements, but do not go on to do in-depth studies. Most of the research is in the form of case studies, historical treatments, and descriptions of community-development activities. There is much emphasis on methods, tactics and approaches to teaching and learning in social movement settings. (260–61)

Researching Social Movement Learning
in the Women's Movement in Chile

Like the objectives of many adult education colleagues, my intent was to expose and explore the phenomenon of political learning in social movements and to draw attention to the educational processes at work within the movement. Chilean women's movements are particularly ideal for such a study. Historically, while confronting structural barriers similar to those faced by women elsewhere in the world, Chilean women have played an important role in their country's social and political struggles (Chaney 1974; Kirkwood 1986). Drawing on this tradition, political mobilization of Chilean women increased sharply in the 1980s despite almost a decade of state repression and rigid economic policies (Agosín 1996; Schild 1994; Valdés and Weinstein 1993; Waylen 1993). "The Chilean case is useful because it had one of the strongest and most successful women's movements in Latin America. The strength, internal coherence and public visibility of the movement helped it to achieve many of its demands" (Franceschet 2001: 208). Some identify the educational and consciousness-raising strategies, now known as the feminist "curriculum" (Valdés and Weinstein 1993), "gender pedagogy" (Quiroz Martin 1997) or "political learning" (Hipsher 1996; Schild 1994), as important factors in this success.

The potential to illuminate the informal political learning processes and the transmission of political knowledge via social movements is highlighted in the Chilean situation because it can be studied through three distinct socio-political periods within three living generations of women with radically different political learning experiences: those who had previously gained the political skills and applied them dauntlessly during the dictatorship, those who were too young to have experienced democracy before participating in anti-dictatorship movements and those who were too young to participate during the dictatorship. How then is social and political knowledge created, transmitted and transformed across these three generations? How has a generation raised during and in the aftermath of a seventeen-year dictatorship affected the ability of civil society to organize and participate in social movements or in a democratic society at all?

As my study progressed, it became apparent that Arica was an especially rich research environment because of its own particular blend of macro and micro politics. The women of Arica, facing danger in a militarized zone at the northern frontier, far from the centre of power in the capital city, were the vanguard of protest against the human rights abuses of the dictatorship. Moreover, Arica characterized a socialist enclave of sorts prior to the military coup.

Research Approaches

Researchers must always select a research approach that matches their research questions and their own philosophies. I was asking questions about the experience of women's political learning in a particular cultural context. A number of assumptions about the social world are embedded in such questions.

First, the way I framed the research questions assumes that people can reflect upon and make meaning of their experiences in the world. This means that the study is *phenomenological.* Phenomenology is the study of people's lived experience and how they make meaning of their experiences. Meaning is what gives form and content to social experiences (van Manen 1990). In this research, I explored the phenomenon of political learning in social movements and searched for the meanings within these human experiences.

A second assumption rooted in the research questions is that contextual factors including culture are relevant for meaning-making. *Ethnography* is a common method used in the social sciences for doing research in diverse socio-cultural contexts. Doing ethnographic fieldwork is the disciplined study of a culture through the eyes of the people themselves (Spradley 1980). "Rather than *studying people,*" Spradley says, "ethnography means *learning from people*" (3). Therefore, I also considered the phenomenon of political learning in relation to the particular socio-cultural context of the women's movement in Arica. As Foley (1999) notes in his study of learning in social movements:

> A powerful phenomenology will give a rich picture of how different people in a situation make sense of it and act on it, and it will seek to make explanatory connections between this micro activity and broader cultural, political and economic processes. A phenomenology is most powerful if it is contextual, if it is *social.* (12)

Finally, the research questions assume that one of these broader social processes is gender (and its relationship to class, race and other forms of oppression). Because social movement participation cannot be adequately understood without a gendered analysis (Alvarez 1990; Jaquette 1989; Miller 1995; Schild 1994; Waylen 2000), I also integrated a feminist approach throughout this research project. *Feminist research* is intended to make visible the experience of women grounded in their everyday reality and to contribute to improvements in their lives. In this research, I highlight women's experiences "as *subjects* — as agents who make choices, have a critical perspective on their own situations, and think and organize collectively against their oppressors" (Mohanty 1991: 29).

Research Methods

Critically investigating phenomena, their meanings and their contextual relationships requires methods that encourage reflection on lived experience. The methods that researchers generally use for these purposes are experiencing (participant observation), enquiring (interviewing) and examining (document analysis). I engaged all of these methods during nine months of fieldwork in Chile from November 2001 to July 2002. For most of that time, I lived with my family in Arica while being hosted for the research project by the feminist NGO, Casa de Encuentro de la Mujer (CEDEMU). During fieldwork, I had countless opportunities for information-gathering. The main source of information for the analysis used in this book is the information obtained from formal and informal interviews with the women's movement participants.

Related specifically to the theme of social movement participation and learning, I conducted twenty-two impromptu, unstructured interviews throughout my travels during the nine months of field work. Often this was with more than one person at a family or social event. Formal interviews included open-ended, in-depth individual interviews and a number of group interviews. I interviewed fifty-three women in a series of thirty-nine group or individual interviews. Two research assistants, each with access to different constituencies within the community, recruited most of the women. In the end, far more women participated in the research than I had originally planned. This was, in part, a case of including "self-appointed informants" (Wolcott 1999). This means that potential interviewees often came forward on their own or were suggested by other women. I decided to interview all the women who wanted to participate as a sign of respect to each of them and of respect to the community. After we conducted a successful pilot group interview, group interviews became the primary vehicle for including larger numbers of interested women.

All the women interviewed had been active in social and political movements in Arica at some time during the previous thirty years. In fact, all the women were involved during the latter years of the dictatorship but few had remained active. Many characteristics of the study population were similar (i.e., gender, geographic location, class), so I purposefully sought variation in age, ethnicity, education and amount and type of social movement experience. The participants ranged in age from twenty-five to seventy-eight with an equal number of women before and after age fifty. The women included activists from all the left/centre parties, the Roman Catholic Church, the community kitchens, the university and the *poblaciones*. Some had held public office and some had lived in exile. Some had long-standing family histories of social/political involvement; others became involved later, sometimes against their family's wishes. Some women were born in Arica; others originated from elsewhere in Chile. Two women self-identified as indigenous but other women born in the north likely had indigenous backgrounds as well. Their educational levels ranged from very little formal schooling to university degrees.

I hired two research assistants from within the community. Sandra Bravo, a member of the CEDEMU team, worked closely with me to arrange and conduct interviews. My bilingual partner, Héctor González, who grew up in Arica, assisted with networking, interviewing, translating and analysis. Together, we translated the original interview guide and then revised it twice more during the course of the interviews. The main topic that we explored in the interviews was the form and context of the woman's participation in social and political movements. Women responded to this topic thoughtfully and thoroughly, typically including information about the learning dimension of their participation in social movements. Once a clear picture of the commonalities across the women's narratives emerged, we developed a separate page of questions that targeted specific areas for follow-up in the last set of interviews. I hired a professional in Santiago to transcribe the interviews.

Analysis in phenomenological research is an ongoing process that occurs concurrently with information-gathering. In this process, analysis moves conceptually between the whole and the parts to look for relationships between the parts that give meaning to the whole. Thus, in order to make sense of social life, analysis is a process of looking for order where none at first glance seems to exist, however tenuous and provisional that "order" may be.

Despite the open-ended nature of the interviews and our concerted efforts to include women whose experiences might contradict the emerging analysis, a distinct pattern of themes emerged early in the research through the repetition of key events, issues and concepts that appeared to be significant for understanding and problematizing learning and education within social movements. Once I recognized these key findings, I combined them into broad themes and then empirically and theoretically elaborated upon them. First, I subjected them to initial analysis in the field through the following methods: The research collaborators and I reviewed the transcripts between interviews and held reflective analysis sessions; after all the interviews were completed, I prepared some analytical themes that we then reviewed with two selected participants; afterwards, we incorporated some of these themes into a final learning/cultural event with all the participants. Second, I sought an explanation of these analytical themes within theories relevant to social movement learning. Last, I returned to the transcripts to see if the analytical themes made sense within the women's narratives. Working from interviews and observations, to the broad themes and related theories, and then back again to the transcripts for empirical authentication reflects the cyclical analytical process described by Agar (1980). In this process, the researcher begins with "large chunks of content" from interviews, observation and documents that seem to have meaning at a broad level and then narrows the focus, building patterns and connections (rather than isolating variables) until there is a "massive over-determination of a pattern" (conference notes, May 5, 2003, see also Agar 1980). The resulting "patterns" are my analytical themes: learning political consciousness, social movement praxis and the consequences of social movement participation.

In phenomenological research, the researcher asks the question: "How do we know that the findings reflect the participant's reality?" In other words, "Did we get the story right?" The most important tools for increasing our level of confidence in the interpretation of the findings are "checking" strategies such as those used in this study. These included multiple interviews, member checks (with CEDEMU team and research collaborators) and collaborating (with CEDEMU and MODEMU). Another method of assuring a comprehensive analysis is often referred to in qualitative research literature as "triangulation." Triangulation is "the use of more than one research technique simultaneously" to increase the opportunity to gather information that might be missed with certain techniques (Cook and Fonow 1990: 82). In this study, triangulation was accomplished through individual and group interviews conducted by three different researchers in combination with participant observation and document review. Immersion and prolonged engagement in the field, regular journal writing and an audit trail (e.g., transcripts, field journals) all contributed to the rigour of the research process.

Ongoing Research

For me, the study of political learning in the women's movement in Chile is a long-term project. For six weeks in January and February 2006, I returned to Arica to share the findings from the original fieldwork, to gather new information on the eve of a presidential election and to explore possibilities for a future project. To this end, I facilitated two focus groups, videotaped two interviews and had numerous informal conversations with participants, research assistants and representatives of the NGO community. Since the emergence of the Penguin Revolution in 2006, I have been working with a Chilean-Canadian research assistant, Alexandra Benitez, to monitor the media coverage and other electronic literature on the movement. Héctor González, now my ongoing research associate in Chile, maintains contact with the women and the NGOs in the community. He also conducted an exploratory interview with two student leaders in September 2007.

6

How Do We Learn
Political Consciousness?

Regarding the organization of women, the trajectory that Arica had as a city was rapid. It was more rapid than in other cities … Why? Because in Arica there was a different political reality than what there was [elsewhere]. In Arica, the left was the majority … and that meant that also there was a greater social organization … [and] a superior level of consciousness.

Introduction

When women in Arica talk about their social movement experience and commitment to social activism, they invariably refer to *conciencia* — consciousness. They talk about political consciousness, social consciousness and civic consciousness. According to the women, they attain this consciousness through political education, social education and conscientization — a term generally attributed to Paulo Freire (2003/1973). Thus, consciousness is crucial in understanding the relationship between social movements and learning/education.

The women describe *conciencia* as a critical social and political consciousness cultivated in their families, their political parties, their communities and their church and embedded in the collective history of a relentless "struggle for rights" in the north and "participation for the common good" during the Allende years. Looking back, the women stressed that *"la izquierda tenía la fuerza de su conciencia"* (the left had the power of its consciousness). For some women, expanding their political consciousness to incorporate a feminist consciousness amplified this effect. Although the women claimed that their activism during the dictatorship years was "necessary," ultimately, it was their "power of consciousness" that motivated them to action.

In the literature on social movements, there is some attention to topics that relate peripherally to the concept of consciousness. Resource Mobilization (RM) theorists often consider questions of recruitment, i.e., who joins movements, why they join and what motivates them to stay even in the face of significant personal costs. Although some theorists criticize RM theory for its lack of attention to consciousness (Carroll 1997; Taylor 1989), the theoretical construct of "collective action frames" offers a potentially productive avenue to explore consciousness within RM theory. According to Klandermans (1997), "collective action frames are sets of collective beliefs that serve to create a state of mind in which participation in collective action appears meaningful" (17). New social movement (NSM) theories are concerned with "processes by which social actors constitute collective identities as a means to create democratic spaces for more autonomous action" (Escobar and

Alvarez 1992: 5). Meaning and ideology are central concerns of NSM theorists. It is common in feminist theorizing about women's movements to concentrate directly on consciousness. In literature about the women's movement in Latin America, for example, the importance of consciousness and consciousness-raising in the mobilization of women is well recognized (see, for example, Alvarez 1990; Miller 1990; Schild 1994; Valdés and Weinstein 1993).

In this chapter, I explicitly deal with consciousness in social movements — what it is and how it is learned.

What is Political Consciousness?

First, it is important to understand the definition of consciousness. Put simply, "our consciousness is comprised of thoughts, ideas and concepts" (Allman 2001b: 33). Thus, a theory of consciousness is a theory of the formation of ideas. How consciousness is formed has been the subject of much philosophical debate. In the 1800s, two contradictory views were held about the origin of consciousness. Hegelian idealism posited that ideas pre-exist independently of the real world and that, in fact, ideas create the real world. Conversely, Feuerbach's mechanical materialism postulated that ideas are the mere recording of the material world. Rejecting both views, Karl Marx contended that ideas originate in our *relationship* with the material world:

> Marx's materialism postulated that ideas and concepts arise from relations between people and from relations between people and their material world.... According to Marx we actively and sensuously experience these relations; therefore, our consciousness is actively produced within our experience of social, material and natural existence. (Allman 2001b: 37)

Within adult education, there is little argument that consciousness entails some sort of interplay between person and society. However, most theories place more significance on one or the other of the personal/social dialectic. For example, one of the most influential theories related to consciousness in North American adult education is Jack Mezirow's (2000; 1990) transformative learning theory. Mezirow theorizes that a form of critical consciousness emerges through the process of challenging taken-for-granted, uncritically assimilated assumptions. However, a number of adult education scholars have criticized the theory for its individualistic orientation (Collard and Law 1989; Collins 1991; Cunningham 1992; Scott 2003). Applying Russian psychologist Len Vygotsky's theory of the social origins and social nature of human consciousness (Wertsch 1985) to transformative learning theory, as has been initiated by Scott (2003), has the potential to add a more social dimension and radical perspective to transformative learning theory.

More typically, however, adult educators interested in political consciousness get their inspiration from Brazilian popular educator Paulo Freire, who in his earliest work describes "problem-posing" education as a means of generating critical consciousness of the material conditions of unjust social structures:

The starting point for organizing the program content of education or political action must be the present, existential, concrete situation, reflecting the aspirations of the people. Utilizing certain basic contradictions, we must pose this existential, concrete, present situation to the people as a problem which challenges them and requires a response — not just at the intellectual level, but at the level of action. (Freire 2003/1973: 95–96)

The interplay between the social and the personal aspects of political consciousness are clearly articulated by feminists. Feminist adult education scholar Mechthild Hart (1990) argues that "consciousness raising is a process of transformative learning because it changes the structure and the frame of experience in general and thus the entire frame of reference within whose parameters the individual woman has been acting so far" (55). She identifies three components to "the full cycle" of consciousness-raising: "the actual experience of power on the individual level, a theoretical grasp of power as a larger social reality, and a practical orientation toward emancipatory action" (70–71). Like Freire, feminists include action in their definition of political consciousness.

The case of the women's movement in Arica provides empirical evidence of this dynamic interaction of the personal and the social in learning political consciousness. This is suggested in linguistic distinctions in Spanish that don't exist in English related to the word *conciencia*. To help me analyze this learning process, I draw on Marx's materialist conception of consciousness as articulated by Antonio Gramsci (1971), Paulo Freire (2003/1973) and Paula Allman (2001a, 2001b, 1995, 1997, 1988).

How is Political Consciousness Learned?

In Spanish, much like in English, people use the noun *conciencia* in combination with a variety of verbs. For example, one can gain *conciencia*, develop *conciencia* or acquire *conciencia*. Unlike in English, however, Spanish also allows for the use of the word "*tomar*" (to take) when referring to consciousness, as in "*tomar de conciencia*." When used in this combination the speaker implies a more active engagement and personal agency in integrating *conciencia* into herself. As such, there is a qualitative difference in the two forms of expression — acquiring vs. taking — that are similar to Freire's (2003/1973) "distinction between being *accessible* to consciousness and *entering* consciousness" (76, emphasis added).

In the remainder of this chapter, I argue that, in terms of learning political consciousness, there is a dynamic relationship between social structures such as family and community that provide the opportunities for "accessibility" to consciousness, and the personal agency of social actors engaging, or "entering," consciousness. Political consciousness is acquired through early learning and integrated through active engagement.

Acquiring Political Consciousness through Early Learning

Early learning within particular social conditions is fundamental to acquiring political consciousness.

The women who participated in the women's movement in Arica typically had early learning experiences from which they began to develop their political consciousness. They were well aware of their historical roots in the mining and indigenous communities in the north of Chile where their ancestors and elders had long ago established a legacy of "the politicization and the organization of the Chilean people." The women traced their consciousness to early memories of implicit values such as fairness, dignity or community concern. "There was always the sense of reciprocity, quite strongly, and of appreciating [people's] worth." Some credited their Catholic upbringing. "The truth is that inside the nun's school, they always gave you values of solidarity and all that business." But most often, women attributed their consciousness to their family's involvement in a political party:

> Why do I have political consciousness? Because… my father worked in a naval shipyard in [a port city], and he had a political cell at his work but they met in my house. Therefore, from very small I knew what political stuff was all about… We saw ourselves involved, so to speak, innocently in the beginning, when we were little, me and my older sister… and unconsciously we found ourselves involved in [political] issues because I have memories from infancy.

Cortez Díaz and Villagra Parra (1999) unveiled this same dynamic in an earlier study of the women's movement in Arica.

> The women began at a very early age to become interested in the political. They were helped by close referents — mother, father, grandparents, etc. — that had some militancy. And they participated in a family dynamic where the political was part of the conversations…. Under those conditions, it wasn't strange that a particular worldview would be shaped in childhood: "I thought that life was like that." (118)

In a Marxist conceptualization, "consciousness is actively produced within our experience of our social, material and natural existence" (Allman 2001b: 37). According to Gramsci (1971), "the child's consciousness is not something 'individual' (still less individuated), it reflects the sector of civil society in which the child participates, and the social relations which are formed within his family, his neighbourhood, his village, etc." (35). Thus, early acquisition of political consciousness is to some extent a passive process that is dependent upon external structural conditions in the child's social environment. In acknowledging the interplay between agency and structure, Coulson and Riddell (1980) argue that the development of social consciousness is not a one-way relationship [of society to individual], but a structured dialectic" (73) wherein "structure is dominant" (80).

Very little adult education literature addresses the possibility that one might acquire a critical consciousness early in life. As suggested earlier, most adult education literature is concerned with the transformation, rather than the formation of consciousness. In Marxist terms, efforts are made to turn false consciousness into critical consciousness. Freire's (2002) stages of consciousness from magical/naive consciousness to critical consciousness are similar to those that Mezirow (1990) draws on to explicate transformative learning among adults.

Yet, for many of the women activists in Arica, their *formation* as critically conscious citizens/women through the teachings and example of significant others (mostly parents) was most striking. This pattern of early political socialization among activists is recognized in many studies about activists. Common to activists is "a continuity of values between their parents and themselves," "early awareness of social and political events, often stimulated by the family's interest and open discussion of these events" and "the influence of individuals other than parents [who are] often themselves activists" (Berman 1997: 69–74). In the student movements in the 1960s in the U.S., "the actions of student radicals were motivated by values learned from their parents" (Marx and McAdam 1994: 88). Among Italian militants, della Porta (1992a) found that "young activists often reflected a continuity with the political traditions of their families" (7). Studying women in the Catholic Worker Movement of the 1930s, Parrish and Taylor (2007) note the "importance of the family environment… in liv[ing] a Catholic faith that included direct, hands-on care for those in need" and the "educational activities offered through the local church" (231). González (1997) demonstrates how, in the Cuban population, a distinct socialist consciousness is established at a very young age through societal values and institutions: "Who I am is a result of my upbringing, my socialization in the context of a revolutionary socialist regime" (64).

In a review of the literature on the emergence of activism, Berman (1997) concludes: "Social consciousness and social responsibility are not behaviors that we need to instill in young people but rather they are behaviors that we need to recognize emerging in them" (39). Lange (2004) arrives at a similar conclusion: when her study participants engaged in a reflective process that resulted in the conscious restoration of values and ethics learned early in life that had been submerged in the frenetic pace of their adult lives, she proposed that incorporating the notion of "restorative" learning would enrich transformative learning theories.

Integrating Political Consciousness through Active Engagement
By actively engaging, or living out, a political consciousness it is deepened and integrated into the self.
The early family- and community-based education that established a set of communitarian values and/or socialist philosophies provided the foundation upon which the women activists in Arica developed, often at a very young age, their *conciencia*. While it was not a wholly conscious experience, it established the predisposition for developing a more robust political consciousness over time. Cortez Díaz and

Villagra Parra (1999) concluded that the first intentions toward activism among the women in Arica were like a quest for spaces to express their "potential capacities for the political life" or their "*ser política*" (political being) (118). Thus, as they entered adolescence, many women made deliberate choices to further expand and act upon their *conciencia*.

All the women became political party members themselves or affiliated themselves with party members. Many became *militantes* (formal members) of the Young Communists. Those who did not have family members in the Communist Party were often introduced to party membership by friends. Still, they recognized that the seeds of their attraction were sown in their families of origin:

> At a very young age, I joined the Young Communists... [I had] the luck to talk to some girls in school that worked in the Young Communists and because in my house they often said that everyone must be respected for who they are, I was introduced to this concept of the equality of people.

As communitarian projects expanded over the years leading up to the election of Salvador Allende as president, women actively participated in many opportunities for democratic citizen participation at the community level, such as the *juntas de vecinos* (neighbourhood councils) and the *centros de madres* (mothers' centres). Some had worked for Allende's campaigns and had established their homes through *tomas de terreno* (land takeovers). Then, "when Allende assumed power, it was like one was acquiring more political consciousness." Likewise, Catholic doctrine during the age of liberation theology was a powerful consciousness-raising tool. "The priest and the nun, in the political part, also told you that we are all equal. I mean, before the society, we all have to be equal." A number of women participated in organizations and activities sponsored by the Catholic Church, through which they could actively put into practice the philosophy of the "church of the poor."

Thus, the idea of *taking* critical consciousness, as it is used in Spanish, implies maturity, action, engagement and agency. In living out one's acquired or "potential" consciousness, *conciencia* is deepened, reinforced and expanded into a "real" consciousness. It is brought to a level of awareness and integration that is only possible through intentional action in the material world. "Real consciousness [is] the result of the multiple obstacles and deviations that the different factors of empirical reality put into opposition and submit for realization by [the] potential consciousness" (Goldman cited in Freire 2003/1973: 113). As Allman states (2001a), ideas or thoughts can "become part of our consciousness when we receive them from an external source... [but] reception depends upon our active engagement with them — an engagement that is, simultaneously, physical and mental" (165-66). Once engaged, this consciousness becomes internalized and subjectified — it is *taken* into oneself.

In the following rhetorical passage, Gramsci (1971) supports the idea of an active engagement in developing one's own "conception of the world":

> Is it better to work out consciously and critically one's own conception of the world and thus, in connection with the labour of one's own brain, choose one's sphere of activity, take an active part in the creation of the history of the world, be one's own guide, refusing to accept passively and supinely from outside the moulding of one's personality? (323)

This "tak[ing] of an active part in the creation of the history of the world" is exactly what the women activists in Arica did. Women believed that they mobilized out of "necessity," that "there was no other alternative." As one said: "For those that had a real consciousness … it was necessary and urgent that things change and the only way was for the people to organize themselves. So, the urgent necessity was to organize ourselves." Ultimately, this "necessity" is the realization and manifestation of a "real" critical consciousness, one that is taken so solidly into oneself that it is "necessary" to act upon. It is this dialectical pairing of a political consciousness with the imperative to act that prompted the women to "go to the streets, every day" despite their fear and the potentially dangerous consequences.

For most women activists in Arica, a collective or socialist consciousness was coupled with an emerging gendered consciousness, adding yet another dimension to their *conciencia*. This was so across Latin America during the dictatorships of the 1970s and 80s:

> In Latin America, a politics of *concientización* has developed in which women have sought to awaken one another's awareness and understanding of their specific historical situation while providing the analytic tools and organizational modes to participate in the transformation of social conditions. … The fusion of a radical critique of economic, political, and social injustice with a gendered analysis has resulted in a syncretic understanding that has transformed both feminism and the politics of social change in Latin America. (Miller 1995: 205)

In part, because the traditional opportunities for men to organize and mobilize during the dictatorship were eliminated, women were thrust to the forefront. Framing their oppositional activities as an extension of their traditional roles in the care and protection of their families, women made political claims from within a "maternalist" discourse.[1] Appropriating this discourse gave them some moral authority and a small measure of safety in expressing their demands. Bringing their personal pain and privation into public view transformed spaces traditionally understood as private into profoundly public domains and redefined what counts as political. For example: "Collective kitchens … are characterized by bringing women together in a public activity replacing the private and almost intimate activity of the kitchen in the domestic sphere. Collective kitchens are the new scenario for women's political work" (Jelin 1990: 189). While some think that the maternal referent may have contributed to the later impasse in women's political participation (Noonan 1995), Franceschet (Okeke-Ihejirika and Franceschet 2002) disagrees, arguing that feminist consciousness-raising "subverted the potentially conservative bases of a maternalist gender ideology," thereby "radicalizing" the discourse at the level of action (459). According to Schild's (1994) analysis of the popular women's movement in Chile, "women have learned to 'know' differently and to act differently" (66). This learning to know differently refers to a changing consciousness — a gendered consciousness. In this sense, some of the women *were* transforming. For a few, the experience was life-changing in the deepest sense, akin to Brookfield's (2000) conceptualization of transformative learning, not simply as a deeper understanding of assumptions as Mezirow (1990) contends, but as "a fundamental reordering of assumptions... a shift in the tectonic plates of one's assumptive clusters" (139).

Some of the women in Arica referred to doors or curtains opening that could never again be closed. The younger women sometimes recognized the influence of their elders in encouraging the development of their own feminist consciousness.

> I began to watch the women leaders... that were working in the whole women's movement. Those women probably didn't realize that we were very much in their hands. We were learning all that they were doing at that time, as the first step, because it was there that they started to talk about the subject of violence, because it was there that they started to talk about the rights of women. The feminist movement here in Arica started to grow, so we were part of that important process and we grew with that and we grew with those images.

While her socialist foundation was not shaken, one of the feminist leaders was transformed through her emerging feminist consciousness, what she calls here the "woman's position":

> There are rebellions that I have always had but today I have them with theory, with practice, with an ideology that is distinct from before. Today, I know why I am like this. I have arguments, I have experience, I have work, I have readings, I have everything that validates [my experience]. Today I have the ability to have a distinct discourse [related to] the issue of women. [But] I tell you that, for me, it's contradictory because neither the political aspect nor the aspect of repression has been as difficult as the ability to assume the woman's position that I have today.

The type of political consciousness that I have discussed in this chapter "is central to an activist's identity" (Klandermans 1997: 112). Women in Arica felt firm in their *conciencia*, adamant that they would never relinquish it, and critical of those who might. For most, their reference is to a socialist consciousness; for others, this is also combined with a new feminist consciousness. Either way, the women experience *conciencia* with the same intensity and integration that Allman (2001a: 170) captures in the following quote:

Authentic and lasting transformations in consciousness can occur only when alternative understandings and values are actually experienced "in depth" — that is, when they are experienced sensuously and subjectively as well as cognitively, or intellectually. In other words, the revolutionary transformations in self... can only come about through a unitary and coherent *deep transformation* or a transformation through which, as Gramsci suggests, knowledge becomes so well "integrated" and "assimilated" that it becomes located within our subjectivities, and thus, in addition to being known, it is felt, or subjectively experienced, as a type of "lived" compassion and commitment. (170)

Upon this solid foundation, the two generations of women activists described in this chapter are powerfully situated to provide the political socialization so critical to developing political consciousness in the next generation. Indeed, they are the mothers and grandmothers of the young activists in the current student movement. Influenced by "both things" — the family and the political party — this new generation is "gaining consciousness" and actively engaging in "the struggle." In the words of a sixteen-year-old Penguins leader who is the president of her secondary school's student association:

I took the position because I realized that my school had many injustices in regards to the rights of the students, many times they were very pressured. Therefore, I saw the need to be here, more than anything, to represent my *compañeros* because for a while now, I have been a member of the Communist Party. So they gave me the initiative and also developed in me a bit more consciousness and so now I have the opportunity to have a position in which I can represent my reality, I accepted it and since then I am one of the leaders here in Arica.

Conclusion

I have demonstrated in this chapter that parents, other family members and communities often introduce the basic elements of a political consciousness based on justice and collectivity in the early years. For political consciousness to be fully realized and integrated, however, engagement by an active subject/agent is required in adolescence or young adulthood. Women activists in Arica had acquired a political consciousness through early learning and had integrated that consciousness through active engagement in political parties, community organizations, the liberatory Catholic Church and anti-dictatorship mobilizing. The formation of a robust political consciousness acted as a buffer and a foundation upon which the women depended even through the challenges to their consciousness that were precipitated by the coup, sustained through the seventeen years of the dictatorship and reinforced by the rampant passivity of the current neo-liberal era.

However, in order for its potential to be fully realized in *sustained* activism, political consciousness must be nurtured and cultivated. Consciousness is not a static phenomenon; it is fragmentary, contradictory and constantly in the process of becoming. New situations, particularly those as traumatically disjunctive from the past as was the case with the military coup in Chile, demand that a political consciousness be constructed and reconstructed through an ongoing and deliberate educational process. This became very apparent in the post-dictatorship era in Chile, when social movement activity and political participation declined and women "returned to their homes." As I argue in the next chapter, without due attention to ideology, the women's political consciousness was not enough to sustain a critical revolutionary praxis into the transition period.

Even so, any "changes in consciousness can have long-term significance because they can serve as a resource for future mobilization" (Taylor 1989: 771). The Penguin Revolution may be that future mobilization.

Note

1. The maternalist nature of women's political participation in Chile was deftly explicated by Elsa Chaney's (1974) study of women politicians. She uses the term "*supermadre*" to signify the expansion of women's mothering role into a larger "*casa.*"

7

What Is Social Movement Praxis?

We wanted to propose a kind of study centre but they wanted to go out into the street ... Our idea was to combine these, that it would have weight, that it would have consciousness, that there would be a space for development and on top of that, we would go out but that we would go out in an organized way.

Introduction

This chapter centres on the meeting of women that was held in Arica on October 29, 1983. During the two years preceding this auspicious meeting, a number of activities organized by women had quietly emerged in Arica that were connected in various ways to the underground activities of the political parties and to the liberation theology of the Catholic Church. In October 1983, a few women "had this idea ... that we would make a larger organization of women ... with all the women of Arica." Subsequently, a small planning meeting was held where invitations to a larger meeting were prepared and defiantly signed. In such repressive times, what the women proposed was extremely risky. Nonetheless, they held fast to their commitment and the meeting was convened.

This meeting, which ultimately launched the women's movement in Arica, was attended by two groups of women. One group was composed of women whose husbands had been detained a few months earlier. Their wives had already occupied the courthouse and orchestrated other demonstrations to publicly denounce the detentions. They urgently wanted to organize women in solidarity and collective protest in order to overthrow the dictatorship. The second group was composed of a handful of leftist women who had started a political study group in the previous year. When they inadvertently discovered a reference to a gathering of Latin American feminists held earlier that year, their mutual experiences of discrimination within their families, their society at large and their political parties fuelled their curiosity about the potential of feminist analysis to advance their political struggles. Hoping to build a larger organization that would prepare women for both the immediate and the long-term struggle, they proposed the meeting. As a consequence of these different objectives, the meeting was fraught with conflict between the two groups. What resulted was not the anticipated unified movement but the formation of two women's organizations, MODEMU and CEDEMU.

By their frequent references to the tension between action and reflection that surfaced in that meeting in October 1983, the women alerted me to the potential of "praxis" as an analytical tool to understand learning in social movements. This tension was apparent in a statement made by a woman in the first group interview in the midst of their shared recollection of the October meeting: "We will get rid of Pinochet and then — what?" Her simple statement embodied the tension between the "getting rid of Pinochet" *actions* and the absence of the *reflection* needed to address the question of "what" would come afterwards.

Adult educators contend that social change requires praxis — a dynamic and simultaneous engagement with both action and reflection. If this is so, then perhaps the polarization of the emerging movement in Arica also polarized these two elements of praxis. In other words, the action/reflection dialectic needed for social change was fractured from the outset. Certainly, this is not the only or defining factor or the sole interpretation of the significance of this meeting; a number of structural, ideological and personal factors interacted in complex and imprecise ways to contribute to a rupture in the women's movement in Arica. In this chapter, I focus theoretically and empirically on the idea of praxis because of its potential to contribute to a better understanding of the educational elements of praxis in social movements. First, I provide an explanation of praxis from a Marxist perspective, and then I explore the expression of praxis in the women's movement in Arica, particularly emphasizing ideological education as an important element in social movement praxis.

What Is Praxis?

The idea of praxis has its roots in early Greek (Aristotelean) philosophy. Later, it became a central tenet of Marxist philosophy in the 1800s when Marx contended that ideas originate in our relationship with the material world. "Basically, [praxis] refers to the human activity by which people shape and are shaped by the world around them" (Youngman 1986: 55). Praxis is a uniquely human phenomenon because human interaction with the environment is conscious and purposive. "The idea of praxis at the level of individual behaviour therefore conceptualises the connection between consciousness and reality, between thought and action" (Youngman 1986: 56). In adult education, we tend to use the terms reflection and action; however, there are many synonyms for these two "internally related" (Allman 2001a) aspects of praxis. For example, thought, theory or consciousness might also signify reflection; practice, production or experience might alternatively signify action. Paulo Freire's well-known phrase "the word and the world" also refers to praxis.

Marx did not intend that we think of action and reflection as polarities. Instead, drawing on a Hegelian dialectical conceptualization, Marx intended to demonstrate that praxis is a dialectical process. As Allman (2001b) explains: "To understand a phenomenon dialectically, or as a unity of opposites, involves conceptualizing it as composed of two parts that are necessary to each other because they could not exist as they currently do without each other" (52). Praxis, then, is the dialectical unity of reflection and action. According to Freire (2003/1973), "Human activity consists of action and reflection: it is praxis; it is transformation of the world. And as praxis, it requires theory to illuminate it. Human activity is theory and practice;

it is reflection and action" (123). Freire underscores this fundamental dialectic by drawing attention to the potential consequences of delinking the two:

> When a word is deprived of its dimension of action, reflection automatically suffers as well; and the word is changed into idle chatter, into *verbalism*.... On the other hand, if action is emphasized exclusively, to the detriment of reflection, the word is converted into *activism*. The latter — action for action's sake — negates the true praxis and makes dialogue impossible. (87–88)

While the notion of praxis in radical education is often assumed to imply a revolutionary or transformative phenomenon, this is a misreading of the basic notion. Rather, as noted above, praxis is the dialectical unity between one's thought and one's action in the material world. There are different kinds of thoughts and different kinds of actions; it follows then that there are different forms of praxis. Allman (2001a) describes the difference between "uncritical reproductive praxis" and "critical revolutionary praxis" as follows:

> If we simply partake in the relations and conditions that we find already existing in the world and assume that these are natural and inevitable — that this is the way things are, always, or at least for a considerable time, have been, and always will be — then our praxis is uncritical and simply reproduces the existing relations.... In contrast, we can choose to question critically the existing relations and conditions and actively seek to transform or abolish them and to create relations and conditions that will lead to a better future for all human beings, in which case our praxis becomes critical or revolutionary praxis as opposed to uncritical/reproductive praxis. (167–68)

A critical revolutionary praxis, then, requires a certain *kind* of reflection. Not only does one need to reflect, one also needs to reflect *critically*. Marx, Gramsci and Freire provide us with ideas about what it means to think critically and, in contrast, how we come to *not* think critically. In brief, "control over... the means of mental production" (Marx cited in Youngman 1986: 67) by oppressors, bourgeois classes or dominant groups intentionally results in the development of "a distorted and partial consciousness that arises from people's lived experience of bourgeois society" (Allman and Wallis 1995: 124) and reproduces ways of thinking (and acting) that serve the dominant class. Marx's critique of bourgeois ideology introduced the notion of false consciousness. Gramsci problematized "the more fragmented forms of popular consciousness, namely the type of consciousness he calls 'common sense'" (Allman and Wallis 1995: 124). Freire (2003/1973) translated the concept into educational terms by likening the dominant educational approach to "banking" — as in an "act of depositing" information or knowledge (72):

The more students work at storing the deposits entrusted to them, the less they develop the critical consciousness which would result from their intervention in the world as transformers of that world. The more completely they accept the passive role imposed on them, the more they tend simply to adapt to the world as it is and to the fragmented view of reality deposited in them.... For the more the oppressed can be led to adapt to that situation, the more easily they can be dominated. (73–74)

In contrast, "the awakening of critical consciousness" necessarily leads to discontent about an oppressive situation (Freire 2003/1973: 34). However, as Allman (2001b) points out, "using concepts critically will not, in itself, change anything. Nevertheless, it is a necessary first step in working out strategies for social transformation" (50). Critical consciousness, or conscientization, "refers to learning to perceive social, political, and economic contradictions, *and* to take action against the oppressive elements of reality" (Freire 2003/1973: 35, emphasis added).

In a dialectical conception, it stands to reason that a particular form of thought would be related to a particular form of action. Integrated with a critical consciousness, critical praxis includes actions that are a "critical intervention in reality" (Freire 2003/1973: 81) and that "transform the relations that constitute the social contradictions" (Allman 2001b: 89).

In sum, a critical praxis, formulated as a unity of reflection and action, is a necessary element of social change.

Clearly, the women activists in Arica had developed a critical political consciousness and were committed to actions that would transform their reality. Does this combination constitute the kind of critical praxis needed for social change? Of course it does. Without doubt, political and social activism is a powerful tool to achieve social change. Furthermore, activism is impossible without some form of reflection. As Allman (2001a) acknowledges, "we do not stop thinking when we act, and thinking itself is a form of action" (167). The women's original route to activism was through their existing social and political consciousness. Movement participation prompted many women to critique and challenge their place in society. They planned their activities, analyzed security issues, evaluated outcomes and formulated strategies. They learned skills, they discussed politics, they used music, theatre and cultural events to raise awareness and, through their public action, they forced others to think about what was happening in the country. The women worked together across political perspectives and social classes and they instituted various initiatives to take full advantage of their collective strength. Women in Arica, as elsewhere, demonstrated amazing courage, determination and creativity in their work toward achieving the downfall of the dictatorship. Thus, dialectically, their actions also offered rich potential for reflection. This dynamic is revealed, for example, in the supermarket scenario wherein the women performed an action that revealed an economic analysis of their material conditions: "We left a symbol as well because not everyone had access to those groceries, only those at some [economic] levels."

Freire (cited in Morrow and Torres 2002) posits that "there is no authentic praxis outside the dialectical unity [of] action-reflection, practice-theory" (134). However, if an "authentic" praxis is difficult to achieve, could this explain why the women's movement could not sustain itself into the transition period despite the women's solid political consciousness, spirited activism and solidarity? Certainly, there is no lack of consequential causes in need of collective action in the post-dictatorship state. What makes an authentic praxis so elusive and how then can it be realized? In the next section, the women themselves provide clues that respond to this question.

The Role of Reflection in Social Movement Praxis: Political Preparation and Ideology

In the early 1980s, a small group of women embarked on an analytical quest, a "study" whose outcome was to be a redefinition of themselves in the world and a redefinition of the world itself. Based on their material circumstances *as women* in an impoverished and terrorizing reality and within political party structures that reproduced the patriarchal relations of the larger society, the women began to think more critically about themselves, their struggle and their society. Through their own practice, these women discovered the value of theorizing, studying and dialoguing as an important complement to their actions. They began to theorize that integrating a socialist analysis with their newly discovered feminist critique held exciting potential for revolutionary practice in their current context. In his chronology of women's movement activities in Chile, Vitale (1996) addresses this phenomenon:

> In [the 1980s], the consciousness of gender combined with an anti-dictatorial political consciousness develops. Previously manipulated by the parties, women start taking control of their right to decide autonomously in the struggle. Under the dictatorship, groups of women were developing that related their specific aspirations with the mobilizations of the Chilean people to end the military dictatorship. (71)

The women who attended the study group were looking beyond the present; they were concerned about planning for the future, for what would happen for women after the dictatorship. The feminist organizers explained:

> We weren't against the idea of working against the dictatorship. Our proposal was to prepare the women. For what? Why? For what would happen after "Pinocho" was out. That was our proposal. That on par with working to get "Pinocho" out, the women would prepare themselves, study… We would analyze this feminist current that we did not consider to be incompatible with what we were doing — it was a different proposal but also liberatory. And what we needed was to maintain a large organization of women for after the tyrant was gone. Because what were we going to do after the tyrant goes? … It wasn't our idea that the women would go back

to their homes. At the time, we thought that the women would capacitate themselves... to have leadership.

"Preparing" and "capacitating" in the ways envisioned here requires time to think, to reflect, to critique and to learn, in a dialectical process that is both informed by action and that also informs action. But for women activists in Arica during the dictatorship, "there was no time to think." Given the "triple duty" of mature women and the inconceivably demanding schedule of young women activists during those years, women had little opportunity for reflective activity. This phenomenon is likely typical of underground movements, as the following excerpt from a summary of various biographical studies attests:

> Many recall the time they spent in the underground as a period of frenetic activism.... The result of this "24-hours-a-day" commitment to the organization was, as one Italian militant put it, the lack of any time for "thinking," for critically reflecting. (della Porta 1992a: 18)

For the women in the struggle, not only was there little time to reflect on *what* they were doing, neither was there time to reflect on *why* they were doing it. It was exactly this concern that prompted one of the leaders to initiate the study concept in the first place:

> I quickly started to be bothered by the orders that came from above that weren't discussed, not even analyzed in your cell ... It was doing things just for the sake of doing them: go out and throw pamphlets, generate a protest, throw rocks at the cops, go and bang on the railings there in [the street], make a fuss, you know. But the truth is that I felt that there was no political formation, none.

The older women who were educated by parents and party elders in socialist and marxist ideology prior to the dictatorship observed that, in contrast, during anti-dictatorship activism, "we didn't prepare ourselves politically." In Arica, as elsewhere in Chile, women effectively united under one objective — to overthrow the dictatorship — and they constructed alliances across ideological lines to achieve it. The lone woman from the Christian Democrats who was a leader in the women's movement in Arica was "rejected by my party because I worked with people from the left." Like others, for her, "the objective was more important than the ideology. We just put the ideology aside." Another concurred, "We forgot about the struggle of the party, we forgot that we were from the Communist Party, the socialist, we struggled as women... We saw nothing more than that this country was burdened with pain."

The younger women complained that, for them, "there was no ideological preparation." They were initiated into politics by their involvement in actions, such as barricades in their neighbourhood streets or strikes on campus, so they were not so well ideologically prepared as the older women who had learned their politics in a less repressive environment. A young woman shared her disappointment:

> I [expected] a process of ideological learning, I mean, like the time when you had to read a lot, to know what the Young Communists are all about, what are the basic principles at least. I believe that not much of this happened... That it was the time to fight and go out into the streets but there was no ideological preparation... There was no solidness, ideological solidness. It was like they threw us to the lions... For me, the Pioneros was a time to prepare oneself to participate in the larger movement and I felt that it wasn't. I mean, for me, it was like that. And the people that were there, that had to prepare me, didn't.

Thus, while the older women worked across ideological lines without preparing themselves politically for women's place in the post-dictatorship society, the younger women complained about not having adequate ideological preparation to sustain their post-dictatorship activism. In the urgency of the times, it seems that a resistance to theory developed within the movement. Cortez Díaz and Villagra Parra (1999) discovered a similar dynamic in an earlier study of the women's movement in Arica wherein there was either a "refusal of political theory" on one hand or a strong demand for political knowledge on the other. In their view, "These extreme positions give an account of what was, or could be in any moment, an alienated practice" (119). Likewise, Moyano (1992) reports that, as Argentinean underground groups became more separated from their political intent, a debate ensued between those who "argued this was time to regroup and develop adequate ideological formulations" and those who "held that [their] strength had always resided in [their] a-theoretical behavior" (117). Holst (2002) suggests that "a turn away from theory toward practice" is characteristic of two generations of the so-called "crisis of Marxism" (3).[1] "A certain hostility to 'theory,'" as Rosa Luxemburg (cited in Holst 2002) pointed out a century ago, "is quite natural for people who run after immediate 'practical' results to want to free themselves from such limitations and to render their practice independent of our 'theory'" (4).

Although there was undeniable strength and effectiveness in the alliances that the elder women in Arica so proudly forged, Gramsci offers a clue to a missing element in the women's movement in Arica that supports the perception of the younger women — the absence of a cohesive ideology:

> The crucial element for Gramsci in holding social movements together was the 'cement' of ideology... Without such theoretical/analytical principles, elements within every social movement only cohere — to borrow Marx's term — like "potatoes in a sack." (Allman and Wallis 1997: 118)

Not surprisingly, Gramsci suggests that a socialist philosophy would make good "cement" for social movements. Such a philosophy would have been familiar to most of the women's movement participants in Arica. Women raised with, educated in and committed to socialism or communism through their families, communities and political parties were favourably situated to take up a critical revolutionary praxis. Those who participated in social actions at the neighbourhood level prior to the coup and those who witnessed the society-changing experiences of the socialist project under Allende had glimpsed the transformative potential of a critical revolutionary praxis. Young women who had heard about the experiences of their parents and who lamented their own lack of "ideological formation" were hungry for a critical revolutionary praxis. Moreover, as the quote below suggests, the women in Arica were well positioned to take up a feminist critique on the solid foundation of the socialist critique. "I believe that my political formation has served me well in upholding my ideological position on the issue of women ... From the ideological point of view, the themes of gender and Marxism [are] coherent in regards to equality."

Thus, few women in the movement would have resisted the "cement" of socialist philosophy and its critical analysis of capitalism. Cementing ideology within a social movement requires a process of critically reflective learning.

Incorporating Ideology into Social Movement Praxis

Adult education scholar Elizabeth Lange (2001) proposes that "critical transformative learning involves a pedagogy of critique (of what is) tempered by a pedagogy of hope (for what could be)" (2). This is similar to Freire's (2004) view that "changing the world implies a dialectical dynamic between denunciation of the dehumanizing situation and the announcing of its being overcome" (62). In this section, I use an analogous approach to demonstrate how a Marxist/socialist ideology might provide the pedagogical framework and foundation for the critical reflection that is required to sustain social movement praxis. I argue that, alongside the actions intended to respond to the immediate crisis of capitalism, social movements are more successful when their members possess the tools to analyze and understand both capitalism and socialism. In a dialectical relationship with activist practice, activists need time and space to reflect upon *capitalist relations* in their current context and upon the *vision* of the socialist society that they wish to create.

Denouncing: Analyzing Capitalist Relations

In order to denounce the dehumanizing conditions of our world, as Freire advises, we must take heed of Marx's advice that we analyze and challenge the *relations* of capitalism, not simply its results. It is well known that the military coup in Chile was a direct result of U.S. interference as part of an obsessive anti-socialist campaign in the region and, correspondingly, as an economic strategy to establish the "neo-liberal laboratory" for the new global economy (see, for example, Chavkin 1985). A Marxist critique suggests that the dictatorship should not be the primary focus of attention. Rather, an analysis of the neo-liberal project would place the immediate result (the dictatorship) squarely within the capitalist system of relations, a system of relations based on economic domination and buttressed by other forms of exploitive relationships (e.g., social, cultural, racial, gendered). Focusing on a result (or symptom) will not fundamentally transform the relations (or cause) from which it emerges. According to Allman (2001b),

> Marx was able to dispel the notion that such antagonisms could be resolved through reforms. He maintained that in such relations one of the opposites depended, for its continuous existence, on a position of advantage.... [The other] can liberate itself from domination and exploitation only by abolishing the relation. (64-65)

In the case of Chile, the goal of removing the dictator is one of reform because the system is left completely intact once the objective is achieved — precisely what happened. Today, the "common enemy" is gone but the relations of capitalism remain securely in place. Based on their research with the women in Arica, Cortez Díaz and Villagra Parra (1999) conclude that the "myth of the common enemy... was confused with the idea of social change" (142). According to Marx, we shouldn't "confuse the starting-point of the struggle and of the revolutionary movement with the goal" (McLellan 1977: 271). How does this confusion arise?

Marx contended that the dialectical contradictions inherent in dominant ideology are masked because they are experienced in different times and spaces. "It is the repeated experience of this tendency that makes it so difficult to mentally grasp these opposites as related" thus giving the distorted perception of a coherent reality (Allman and Wallis 1995: 124). In Gramscian terms, this becomes "common sense," a taken-for-granted fragmented popular consciousness.

In the final years of the military regime, various coalitions were formed to pressure for an end to the dictatorship and later, to negotiate the "transition to democracy." As the negotiations proceeded, a moderating process occurred. Through a left-centre alliance, the Concertación por la Democracia (Coalition for Democracy) was formed that fortified relations with the Christian Democratic Party (in which certain factions remained aligned with Pinochet) and excluded the Communist and other far left parties. In return for winning the "return to democracy," the negotiating Concertación accepted a transition pact that included an agreement to retain the neo-liberal economic model previously imposed through force. Such political strategies, "while making significant demands within the confines of liberal democracy, do not move us beyond capitalism. ... Capitalism deflects struggles away from itself and toward the expansion of democracy" (Burawoy cited in Holst 2002: 46).

Therefore, while Chileans were desperately struggling to regain "democracy," capitalism's reach was quietly solidified and any possibility for socialism was pushed definitively off the agenda through the consolidation of neo-liberal economic policies. A now obvious contradiction was not immediately apparent because ousting the dictatorship was "naturally" equated as a return to democracy and, in turn, a return to democracy "naturally" implied a return to socialism (common sense thinking). Thus, by separating democracy from socialism in the transition period, it was some time before the real impact of a reformist agenda became apparent, that is, neo-liberalism severely restricts the possibilities for an effective democracy. Even though Chile has elected a "socialist" president for the past two terms, almost two decades after the dictatorship the irresolvable contradictions between the neo-liberal economic model and the democratic process are undeniable (see, for example, Bresnahan 2003).

Pedagogical spaces intentionally inserted into or uncovered from within social movements allow opportunities for analyzing capitalist relations in a process informed by activists' material and practical experience. The neo-liberal laboratory in which they lived required a counterpart in an analysis of neo-liberalism (and the associated relations of domination). Both the laboratory and the analysis are educational activities — the laboratory being the site of learning through experimenting with altered (and profoundly unjust) material conditions and the analysis being the required reciprocal activity of learning through the critical analysis of those material conditions. "The political explanation of concrete problems in struggle is radical adult education" (Holst 2002: 113). Both resistance actions and reform measures that are activated to get rid of the dictator, then, are recognized as preliminary moments in the larger project of tackling neo-liberalism, and the actions that follow the fall of the dictatorship are informed by this broader analysis. On the significance of analyzing capitalist relations in anti-dictatorship activism, Assheton-Smith (personal correspondence, March 10, 2004) reflects: "The notion within the theory is that if you have a solid political and economic analysis, you will know that falling [sic] the dictator will not solve your problems, but be barely a baby step in moving forward. You will probably correctly predict ways that the 'revolution' could be lost after his fall, and the critical importance of certain kinds of steps."

This is precisely the reason that a "pedagogy of critique" is necessary in a critical revolutionary praxis. However, this praxis is incomplete without a vision to further guide activist practice in the post-dictatorship era.

Announcing: Clarifying the Vision

For Freire, announcing how things could be once we have overcome the injustice of dehumanizing conditions is the "dream." "Dreams are visions for which one fights" (Freire 2004: 32). Vision is an image or a concept in the imagination that anticipates the future. Thus, visioning is a reflective process. Along with Freire, radical adult educator Paula Allman (2001b) is adamant about the significance of vision in a "process of social transformation" (7). She argues that collective dialogue, debate and struggle are necessary to achieve a sustainable, shared and cohesive vision about the meaning of socialism and social transformation that is capable of generating lasting social change.

> If we are going to create a more humanized form of existence, we need at least a broad notion of what this would entail.... I make no claims that overcoming capitalism and other aspects of injustice and oppression will be easier given a clearer vision of what we might be trying to create. However, I cannot understand how we can get anywhere without a clear and realistic vision. (9–10)

Reiterating Freire's principles of moral philosophy, Morrow and Torres (2002) include one principle related to the concept of vision: "We ought (collectively and dialogically) to consider what kind of world — what social structures, processes, relationships, and so on — would be necessary to enable (all) people in a given social setting to pursue their humanization" (104). Vision, according to Allman (2001b), is neither totalitarian nor utopian.

> It is primarily an expression of values rather than a blueprint, as the latter would thwart the creative intervention of human beings. This creative intervention is one of the — if not the — most fundamental values in Marx's vision; therefore, a blueprint would be sheer hypocrisy.... Any vision worth striving for must be realistic rather than whimsical. It must be based on considerations and critiques of the past and present human condition. In other words, to be achievable, a vision must be derived from the real, the material world. (7–9)

In Arica, the women struggled to rid themselves of the military regime without a vision of what should follow. One of the underground leaders voiced a regret shared by others.

> It's frustrating... we committed a grave error. We worked exclusively to overthrow [the dictatorship], so that Pinochet would be gone. But we did not make a definite alternative of what to do after that. I believe, also, that is the cost we are paying. Even having so many great minds, we still didn't accomplish anything.

Many of the elder women envisioned that the socialist project started by President Allende would automatically resume:

> I thought that it was going to be something that looked more or less like the time of Allende, that we were going to continue the same, with the same rights for the workers, the same opportunity for everyone to work... So we all had hope that it would again be like before, nothing more.

The younger women did not project even a shadowy vision of the future. One young woman articulated this comparison: "I lived all my life in the dictatorship... I don't know how to live in a democracy. [The older women] know the difference between democracy and dictatorship."

One woman reflected, "We thought that democracy was going to return and recuperate everything... I think that the expectations were too high." On the contrary, their expectations may not have been high enough. Holst (2002), for example, suggests that the Chilean left may not have been "revolutionary enough" during the Allende years "in the sense that it did not do away with the right's hold on the military" (72). Or perhaps the women's expectations were not formulated clearly enough. The clearest objective was an *absence* of something (the dictator) rather than a solid notion of the *creation* of something (democracy/socialism) that could guide a more critically nuanced form of activist practice. Feeling despair over the current neo-liberal system in Chile, women asked themselves: "Why did we struggle so much to have a democracy? For what? For this? This is what we were searching for?"

Summary

A meeting held in October 1983 signalled the emergence of the women's movement in Arica into two philosophically distinct women's organizations, MODEMU and CEDEMU, which in turn fractured the action/reflection dialectic needed for social change. The women were left without a clear analysis of their socio-political situation or a vision for what should follow. Since the elections of 1990, most of the older women have returned to their homes and to their previous lives. Typically, the younger women whose formative years were framed by both the dictatorship and the struggle have opted out of socio-political activism in disillusionment and disappointment. In retrospect, some women wonder if the division of the movement and the lack of a "study" component was a strategic error. To their dismay, they realize now that, because the question "then what?" was never addressed during the anti-dictatorship struggle, they were ill prepared to contribute to shaping a post-dictatorship future. Praxis was inhibited in this instance by a lack of an "explicit curriculum" (Youngman 1986: 106) that would combine a critical analysis of the relations of capitalism (as symbolized by the dictatorship) with a concrete vision of the future. "A pedagogy of critique and a pedagogy of hope" (Lange 2001) incorporating both critical analysis and vision, denouncing and announcing (Freire 2004), might provide the reflective practice needed to inform new actions for the current, but hardly less traumatic, capitalist era in Chile and elsewhere.

Note

1. Holst is referring here to parallels between the crisis of Marxism occurring at the end of the nineteenth and twentieth centuries.

8

How Does Participating in Social Movements Change Lives?

I believe that the dictatorship changed us. I mean, I believe that for us there is no other change. I believe it was so strong, it was so many years, that it is difficult to change again. What could be so big or so terrible that it could make me change more? I mean, one rebuilds maybe in terms of new scenarios but at the bottom, you are already a different person. I mean, you will never be the same.

Introduction

What happened to the women of Arica who risked everything to depose Pinochet? Women who participated in the women's movement in Arica were affected by their anti-dictatorship activism in different ways. At the time of the coup in 1973, most of the women in the older cohort were already adults, no longer studying and already married. They had been ideologically educated in more politically open times. After 1989, they returned to their homes and families, albeit with new understandings, strengths and convictions. "The dictatorship did us a favour in that sense because it liberated us. I, for one, was stuck in the house all my life. So women became more independent… and learned to value [themselves] more." For most, the anti-dicta-torship struggle was both traumatic and liberating but the effect was tempered by the social roles, life experiences and responsibilities associated with their stage in life.

In contrast, in 1973, the women in the younger group were not yet born, were children or were young adolescents. These women lived their formative years in the contradictory reality of repression and resistance from which they learned their world, defined their citizenship and forged their identities. "I was raised in the dictatorship. I was born in the dictatorship… The dictatorship formed me." Being suddenly jettisoned into politics without political preparation, they were not as strongly situated ideologically as the older women.

In the social movement literature, there is very little attention given to the personal and social consequences of social movement participation — positive or negative — and this is especially so for underground or clandestine movements (della Porta 1992a). Simply, a "consequence" is something that follows as a result. In the language of the women activists in Arica, consequences are those things that "marked" them (*me marcó*) as a result of their social movement experience. When a woman speaks of being "marked," she identifies two types of consequential experi-ences: those that "taught me" (*me enseñó*) and those that "cost me" (*me costó*). The positive learnings that resulted from the social movement participation of women activists in Arica included solidarity, women's empowerment and skill development. However, the women also experienced painful negative consequences, both individual and collective. The costs — *las heridas* (the wounds), *las secuelas* (the sequelae) and *los dolores* (the pain) — of social movement participation emerged most often in the stories of the younger women who were adolescents and young adults during anti-dictatorship activism. From 1983 to 1989, young women's involvement in social movements was extensive: from the church, human rights, cultural and women's/ feminist activities to neighbourhood barricades, graffiti brigades and campus strikes. The brutal military and economic repression during the dictatorship combined with the solidarity and courage of the resistance movements incontrovertibly shaped the younger women, influencing who they became.

In this chapter, I focus particularly on the learning and development of *las jóvenes*, the twenty-two younger activists in the women's movement. Because of the formative nature of experience at this stage of human social development, it is especially fitting to consider their experience from a learning perspective. In the first part, I chronicle the unique experiences of these younger women. In the second part, I draw from other social movement studies and related literature to examine the helpful and harmful consequences of social movement participation on social/ political and personal/interpersonal lives and to explore the effect of emotions and trauma on social activists.

Las Jóvenes: The Lost Generation

One realizes the complications of wars, the cost of wars. It's true that we had an internal war here. It wasn't a war with another country. So, it was more painful because it was with our brothers and sisters. And you also realize that, in a war, everyone loses, nobody wins. Everyone loses dreams, loses life, everyone loses. You lose your identity, your life, your *compañeros...* The women of our degeneration [the young woman laughs at her play on words], our generation have been a very damaged generation. We are the lost generation.

La generación perdida. The lost generation. A generation defined by loss/es. This is the legacy of seventeen years of a military dictatorship and an equal number of years of unfulfilled expectations. The terrorizing military environment unquestionably affected the overall development —social, emotional and intellectual — of *las jóvenes*. The military infiltrated the population by living in civilian neighbourhoods in large numbers. What's more, "there were informers around every corner. You had to watch your back, you didn't know if your friend was an informer." Fear, suspicion and "generalized distrust" permeated their environment, reinforced through visible and menacing military might; to see or to hear tanks, soldiers, police, dogs, shooting and black-outs were common. Even more intimidating were the ever-escalating numbers of detentions, tortures, disappearances and deaths of parents, other family members, friends and neighbours. In this crippling environment of fear, even an innocent walk to school was accompanied by "a state of terror."

> When I was in grade school, I remember well, when I was walking with my sister on the way to school and in the main street here, that is Tucapél, all the people were protesting and the military were doing something to them. A little kid confronting that situation... [had] zero protection. And you didn't have another option because you had to go to school because if you didn't go to school, the military would come looking for you at the house. So, it was an order that no matter what, everyone had to go to school. So, in the end, you went to school and you faced up to that sensation of danger.

Once in the classroom, children were exposed to an educational curriculum drastically altered to reflect the "official" version of history. As one woman reported, "the history books that we read were the books made by the right... 'Chile is a militarized country where the Father of the Country is a military person that is a dictator.'" Moreover, the military coup was not mentioned: "The history books that tell you about 1973 are very few." In order to eradicate any reference to popular or socialist thought, books were burned, libraries were destroyed and teachers and university professors sympathetic to the left were fired, exiled or disappeared. The military government strictly controlled all sources of information, including the mass media, and tolerated no sources of alternative discourse.

Because of her choice to be involved in clandestine or prohibited activities, a young woman's educational studies were often delayed or curtailed, leaving her educational potential unrealized. One young woman discussed the educational discrimination that young activists faced in secondary school:

> There was a lot of mistreatment when the teachers caught on that you were [involved] in political activity, some teachers from the right. They mistreated you with grades, and you had to fight for your grades and you had to fight for your tests. [You said to them,] "show me the tests." I remember one civics teacher who hid the tests from me and he wouldn't give them to me because he knew I was from the left. So there was a certain struggle that you had as a student.

At the university, students demonstrated collective resistance to academic repression and control by striking, protesting and occupying the campus. During classes and while writing exams, students were fearful of reprisals that came without warning.

Vastly different from the tragedy of 1973, 1983 was a watershed year throughout the country for the mass mobilization of resistance movements. By the late 1970s, when the economic hardships had escalated beyond endurance, survival initiatives were organized by women, human rights groups were established and political parties were quietly rearticulating. At this point in their lives, *las jóvenes* (half of

97

whom were eighteen and over by this time) began to witness resistance, solidarity and courage. In many cases, young girls saw their mothers, fellow students and *vecinas* (neighbours) in action. Children played the "cops and protesters" game in a re-enactment of what they witnessed around them. One young woman, babysitting for movement leaders, recalled "I began to watch the women… I was young and I looked after the children of these women that were working in the whole women's movement." Sometimes, daughters encouraged their mothers to participate, as in the situation where a mother joined the movement to reduce her anxiety about her children's involvement and in the example of a young woman convincing her mother to participate in a demonstration called a *cacerolazo*. "And from that moment, she made a commitment to accompany me to the demonstrations. She also made a fuss, spoke out in public and we went together like that to many things."

Some of the younger women participated despite their family's disapproval. One young woman married into a communist family who introduced her to political activities, setting her anti-communist family against her. Subsequently, she didn't see them for five years even though she lived in the same city. Seven years younger, another woman was not yet in a position to openly defy her parents' political position. So, while her parents assumed she was asleep in her room, she secretly left the house.

> I escaped over the roof for God's sakes! I waited in my house. It was very comical… At my mother's first snores, I took off the blankets. I was wearing jeans, t-shirt, socks and had my runners at hand. I fished out my runners and I hung them around my neck. I climbed a railing that's there, a wall in my house that goes from the back of the patio to the street. And from there, like the *Circus of the Montini's* [TV show] nowadays, I ran and jumped down, put on my runners and left.

Women said that "the young were riskier, bolder" and that "the women were bolder and braver." So, being women *and* being young, *las jóvenes* were indomitable. They took risks with their lives almost daily, engaging in both public and clandestine activities. By definition, clandestine work required that identity be protected. The young activists often wore balaclavas or handkerchiefs as they occupied the barricades or incited the crowd with megaphones from the back of a truck. In hindsight, women laughed about the incongruence of this practice because they were recognizable anyway: "Everyone knew my butt" or "Where is A. or S. going to hide with a voice like that?"

Even the very youngest children who were "raised under the tables" of political meetings and activities sometimes had an important role to play. In one situation, a mother put political pamphlets under her five-year-old daughter's pillow just as the military arrived at the house and two mothers described hiding documents in their daughters' diapers.

For *las jóvenes*, the exposure to feminism was simultaneous with their involvement in leftist movements. Even the youngest had witnessed or experienced sexism in the political parties and labour movements. Women activists believed that their commitment and exposure to danger was more than equal to men's. Young women made comments such as "there were always more women than men," "the woman was always in front" and "she was like a core of the political movement." Yet, they felt undervalued as women. They recognized that women did not hold positions of power in the same numbers as men, that women did not make the final decisions, that women were "excluded" from the "special work" of men, that women's political work was "taking messages" and "making tea" — that fundamentally, leftist organizations were "*machista*." The women also began to reflect on their experiences in their own families where they saw fathers in charge and brothers with rights, responsibilities and expectations that were different from their own. *Las jóvenes* developed into womanhood alongside second-wave feminism, from which they gained a clear *perspectiva de género* (gender perspective). "We were part of that important process and we grew with that, we grew with those images." One university student recalled an event organized by women students that put those images into practice, even though they were in direct conflict with a Communist Party directive.

> We took the university one day. [Afterwards], they called us to task for being inconsistent, that the gender struggle was sort of insignificant beside the democratic struggle for the country. But for us, it was the same. I mean, if we fought for a democratic space it wasn't only so that the men could make the discourse or rise to political posts. We understood democracy as a democracy also for us, a democracy of relations, of more democratic relations.

Most of the younger women hold feminism as integral to their current philosophical framework.

> The majority of us ended up in feminist groups or tried to learn more about feminism. And one way or another, through different routes, we arrived at feminism. I tell you, the majority. I mean, I don't know even one that hasn't gone this route.

Of particularly lasting importance to these women was their growing awareness of alternative roles for women in Chilean society. One woman, now in a long-term committed relationship, suggested that "today the women of the left have an advantage, that the whole process that we lived permitted us, those of us that have partners, to establish couples in much more egalitarian terms, [to be] much more committed." However, she added, "few can take advantage of it because few women today have a partner." Many women activists of her generation are alone, separated from their husbands and rarely in a stable relationship.

Drawing on Sonia Montecino's (1996) analysis of Latin American/Chilean gender identity, one woman offered an explanation. She said that the women of her generation are "screwed" for having challenged, through the strength of their movement activities and leadership as well as their obligatory entry into the labour market during the dictatorship years, the "prototypical" Chilean woman, that is, the submissive and selflessly giving Virgin Mary. While the women grew in a sense of their own worth and capabilities, however, many men remained behind, "stuck and stagnant," threatened and unsure of how to react to this reconstruction of the Chilean woman. "They are no longer the *machos*, I mean we women can go forward and we can do many things." But this came at a price: "It has brought conflicts in our couple relations." As one woman observed, "Today, without that ideal or fear that united them before, they have separated." For many couples, once the all-consuming commitment to a mutual objective that had absorbed their energy and focus during the dictatorship years was no longer present, little was left to sustain a relationship that had been put aside for so long. "It came to an end, that common theme that united you to your *compañero* — the struggle. Day after day, that was what we did … The dictatorship ended, and all the marriages began to end. We lost many things in relation to the couple because you didn't build anything together."

Most of *las jóvenes* delayed having children. Many, unlike their mothers, have only one or two children. Some have children later than other women of the same generation and some choose to have children outside of a committed relationship. "Many people didn't have children either, because to have children was dangerous and to have children was to take away time from your political activity." Overall, one woman concluded, "It was an epoch of postponements. Postponing the family, the studies, the children."

Young women also speculated about the long-term learned effects of political, systemic violence on themselves, their children and families. A young psychologist expressed concern about the "damaging" effects that the dictatorship had on the people of Chile: drug and alcohol addiction, disconnected families, depression and abuse. Some women spoke about the deep pain and loss they experienced even from witnessing the pain of others. One young woman travelled for one month with the *madres* from the Santiago Association of the Relatives of Disappeared Detainees. "I cried for just about the whole month with those women because … those women lost their children … After being out with them, I was sick for about fifteen days because it seemed like I had absorbed [their pain]." Many spoke about imprinted fear responses. "One is fearful, very fearful because they taught us to have fear. We lived in a regimen of fear." The psychologist hypothesized that the repression that Chileans experienced during the military regime has created an unhealthy "punishment-oriented society" that is prone to high levels of woman and child abuse. Some further supposed that the dictatorship's immunity from prosecution sends a message to people that violence is tolerated and goes unpunished. From the perspective of a woman who was an underground human rights worker during the dictatorship:

> Today, we have the latent cruelty of the dictatorship, what it did to us. It destroyed us completely. It killed our solidarity. It killed the humanity that

had been inside every Chilean … This horror that the dictatorship imposed on us began to kill us definitively.

The younger women managed a gruelling schedule of anti-dictatorship activities that left no time for anything else. Afterwards, many felt used, manipulated and betrayed. "It was like they threw us to the lions," said one. One young woman expelled from the Young Communists when she openly disagreed with a directive, expressed such feelings:

> I did things with a lot of heart. I believed in what I was doing and we risked our life every time we did a dangerous action … When I realized how things functioned internally, I didn't like them. I felt a bit cheated, manipulated. And when they threw me out, of course I felt very hurt because I had done so many things.

Other young women mourned "the giving, the surrendering, the risking everything for everything and, in the end, being left empty" or "doing and doing and doing and then it's like you're left with nothing." This nothingness or emptiness includes personal losses as well as debilitating disillusionment and depression after having fought so hard to gain so little. "I did not fight for this!" wrote one young woman in a poem, "Our struggle was in vain … How many youth wasted, how much faith lost, how much sadness and disillusionment." Unlike the older women who were unequivocal in their belief that they would do it all again despite the outcome and the costs, the younger women seemed less certain. Some openly speculated, "If I had questioned it, maybe I wouldn't have gone out" or "If I analyze it now, I tell you, I would never do it again."

While most were no longer engaged actively in political parties or social movements, none of these women had rejected the political consciousness that had developed from their families and/or through their movement involvement. Most expressed their social commitment through their chosen professions or jobs. Among these women were:

- teachers or early childhood educators who hoped to have a positive influence on the upcoming generation;
- popular educators, counsellors or social workers who worked with troubled youth and families, addicts and abused women;
- community and feminist organizers and activists; and
- visual, text and performance artists who communicated educational messages and social critique through their creative work.

No longer active in a political party, a theatre artist reflected upon the form of her political participation today:

> For me it is sort of primordial to put something forward, to put forward

different visions to the community... Through what I do, which is theatre, I can give that to the people. I can tell them, "Hey, wake up." Maybe tell them that they are sleeping. I believe that one can produce movement, one can make the people move... That is the most important thing. I belong now to [a cultural] collective. That is also important to me. It is opening the doors to put something forward to other women.

Despite the consequences imposed on them by the dictatorship, most of the women remain pragmatic. As one said of the end of the era, "I separated. I cried. I had to reconstruct my life again, I mean, I had to begin to live again in another form." Another said, "The process of learning is contradictory... I take out the positive but the negative I leave behind." Younger women talked often about regrouping on a more personal level, within their homes and families and within themselves as well. One talked about the "preliminary work" that is needed and another about "begin[ning] to change the person to construct a different way of life... [because] the society is constructed through a new person." Some women appreciated the help of the social organizations such as CEDEMU and SERPAJ in their healing and learning processes. "SERPAJ has helped me... to have a fuller vision, more diverse, more integral, more human... So, I believe that it has helped me to be more sane than contaminated."

Mothers felt strongly about their maternal role in constructing a different society. One young mother hopes to give her daughter a "solid foundation" of ideology, values, ethics and habits from which to grow. Another hopes that her daughter "always holds her head high, that she is always clear and true to her principles, that she speaks the truth." A third wants her daughter to "understand not to ever repeat the atrocities that we lived, not here nor in any neighbouring country, nor in any part of the world."

In spite of the catastrophic upheaval of those years of struggle, all the women treasured solidarity, collective action and the power in mutual commitment. For *las jóvenes*, solidarity signifies intimate friendships fashioned from "a complicity and a history. We have forged a history in the skin. So that unites us." When asked how her involvement in social movements influenced her, a young woman replied:

> It changed my life because in that social movement, one got to know what solidarity really is, to know what *compañerismo* is... One gets to know friends, I mean they are not friends, they are good *compañeros* — something more profound. Because... they are the people with whom you share life and death. They are the *compañeros* that one day you had to run and a *compañero* caught your hand and you ran harder.

In many ways, both positive and negative, the repression and the resistance changed the path of *las jóvenes* potential lives, individually and collectively:

> It has been a change at the level of the masses, collectively. Also, it was a change at the personal level. Why? Because in that time, I was very young,

I was finishing my studies. I had a plan for my life. I had said, "I am going to do this and this." I couldn't ever do that because I had to change those plans for others. First to defend life, to see how we were going to organize ourselves to confront this.

These young women conveyed a sense of disorientation, of unfulfilled potential, of a future stolen, of a generation lost. "Many times I ask the question, 'if that hadn't happened in this country in 1973, what destiny would I have had today?'"

Consequences of Social Movement Participation

Of the positive consequences related to participation in the Latin American women's movement, the findings from my study are congruent with a wealth of other studies and literature. However, a number of other consequences that emerged in this research have not been well studied in social movements. In this part of the chapter, I draw from diverse literatures that may contribute to understanding three sets of consequences that are experienced in the lives of the younger women activists in Arica.

First, *las jóvenes* retained the political consciousness that they had cultivated through social movement activism during the dictatorship years. Yet because this nascent consciousness was not adequately developed into a solid ideology, they were left with an ideological void that made it difficult for them to maintain their involvement after the dictatorship. (See Chapter 7 for a discussion of the role of ideology in social movement praxis.) Their established political consciousness coupled with this ideological void has had distinctive effects on their *social and political lives.*

Second, the younger women's social movement experiences are also deeply imprinted on their marital and childbearing biographies as well as on their education and work biographies. In other words, they have experienced significant consequences in their *personal and interpersonal lives.*

Third, the contradictory environment of repression and resistance during the dictatorship generated *emotions* and produced *trauma* that have an enduring impact on all aspects of the lives of *las jóvenes.*

Consequences in Social and Political Lives

In this section, I consider the consequences of social movement participation on the younger women's social and political lives through two topics: political commitments and ideologies, and social movement continuity. In these topics, the activist experience in Arica is consistent with findings from other social movement studies.

Political Commitments and Ideologies

As described in the previous section, the political views and sympathies held by *las jóvenes* in the 1980s have endured into the new millennium and continue to impact their personal, relational, political and professional commitments.

Contradicting the widespread (and media reinforced) image of the 1960s-era activist turned "opportunistic yuppie" (McAdam 1989), empirical studies of U.S. activists have consistently found that former activists retain their ideological stance over time and remain politically involved. While there may have been a "softening" or "moderating" of some extreme positions, activists had "held on to their essential beliefs" (Marwell, Aiken and Demerath III 1987: 374), had moved more to the left in orientation after their initial activist experiences, tended to remain active in other social movements, and had maintained networks and relationships developed during their activist experiences that often reinforced later activism (McAdam 1989). Looking at gender differences, McAdam (1992) found that, compared to men, women perceived that their activist experience in an early civil rights activity called "Freedom Summer" had a greater positive impact on their subsequent political beliefs and commitments.

Studying feminist activists in the U.S., Whittier (1995) concluded:

> Veterans of the 1970s women's movement had been transformed by their experience. They could not simply turn away from their politics and step back into mainstream society... [C]ommitment to social change remains central to their sense of themselves, their peers, and the world as a political place. For core members this commitment has been exceedingly enduring. (80–81)

Recent research from Chile suggests that while social activists in the Santiago *poblaciones* may have become cynical, disillusioned and disengaged from the institutionalized political system (such as political party membership and voting), they are neither apolitical nor de-politicized.

> Various degrees of class consciousness and critical political awareness are still present among sectors of the *pobladores....* There is a clear, precise, and acute consciousness of the shift in formal politics, the limitations of the transition, and the decline in participation since 1990 as a consequence. (Olavarría 2003: 31–32)

Despite holding a strong political consciousness, the lack of a solid ideological grounding (see Chapter 7) has made it difficult for women to coalesce around new goals and objectives. This same concern about an "ideological void" arose in Olavarría's study (2003) of present-day social activists in Santiago's *poblaciones*, who complain of "no education in political militancy" (22) and "no ideological discussion" (26). Like *las jóvenes* in Arica, the Santiago activists also make comparisons to earlier days, prior to the dictatorship, when there existed political discussion and "education of the cadre" (22). Moyano's (1992) findings from her study on the Argentinean underground suggest similar concerns regarding inadequate "ideological formulations" that ultimately affected the movement's strategy choices.

Social Movement Continuity

Although they have generally retreated from political parties, the younger women activists have maintained numerous informal social and political connections. Many of the younger women participate with their elders in CEDEMU and/or Mujeres de Luto, two remnants of the women's movement from the dictatorship era.

Taylor's (1989) study of the continuity between the first-wave and second-wave feminist movements in the United States contradicts what she calls the "immaculate conception" view of the social movements of the 1960s. Instead, she suggests that these movements can be "viewed as a resurgent challenge with roots in an earlier cycle of feminist activism" and that, in between the resurgence and the roots, there existed "a holding process by which movements sustain themselves in nonreceptive political environments and provide continuity from one stage of mobilization to another" (761). Building on Taylor's work, Whittier (1995) investigated the "persistence" of the women's movement into the decidedly anti-feminist climate that followed second-wave feminism in the U.S. She concluded, "Both generational politics and the hostile climate of the 1980s affected the course of the women's movement, but neither caused its demise" (5). Rather, through the combination of longtime and incoming feminists, the movement was sustained and transformed, surviving mostly at the grassroots — within smaller women's organizations and integrated into personal and political lives. Taylor's (1989) concept of abeyance is useful in considering the role of spaces such as CEDEMU and Mujeres de Luto that preserve the movement in quiescent times:

> A movement in abeyance becomes a cadre of activists who create or find a niche for themselves. Such groups may have little impact in their own time.... The significance of abeyance lies in its linkages between one upsurge in activism and another.... Abeyance structures perform this linkage function through promoting survival of activist networks, sustaining a repertoire of goals and tactics, and promoting a collective identity that offers participants a sense of mission and moral purpose. (762)

The notion of continuity also appears in the study of youth movements. In a review of five "historical generations" of youth movements spanning 200 years, Braungart and Braungart (1993) concluded that youth movements "have been at the forefront of defining, redefining, and extending the concept of citizenship" (170) "in waves during certain periods in modern history... representing combinations of generational and historical forces" (139). They suggest that youth may occasionally assume a "generational mission" to reconstruct social values (170). These authors include Latin America in three of the identified generations of youth movements: in the 1930s and again in the 1980s, the focus was economic crises and political repression; in the 1960s, U.S. imperialism and economic inequities inspired by the Cuban revolution and liberation theology ignited youth protest. The Penguins in Chile may signify the next of these waves.

Consequences on Personal and Interpersonal Lives

Numerous demographic studies conducted over the past twenty-five years have investigated the "biographical consequences" of participants who were active in social movements in the U.S. during the 1960s. These studies have revealed that the personal and interpersonal lives of political activists are affected by early activism on a number of dimensions that coincide with the activist experience in Arica. While these studies are flawed in making no connection to either the societal impact of these biographical consequences or to the current sociopolitical context in which they are embedded, they are instructive at the micro level.

First, the younger activists in Arica clearly identified a different marital and childbearing biography than others of their age. Many then entering mid-life were single (never married or separated) and tended to have fewer children later in life than others their age. A review of the literature on social movement activists suggests that they were more likely to remain unmarried or to marry late, to be separated or divorced and, if they had any at all, to have had fewer children later in life (Klandermans 1997; Marwell, Demerath III and Aiken 1993; McAdam 1989; Van Dyke, McAdam and Wilhelm 2000).[1] Studies of gender differences have indicated that to a higher degree than men, activist women were more likely to be unmarried than non-activists (although the timing of marriage was not affected) (Van Dyke et al. 2000) and the decreased likelihood of having children seemed to be more true for women than for men (Marwell et al. 1993; Van Dyke et al. 2000). Cortez Díaz and Villagra Parra (1999) found that the Arica activists hesitated in making decisions about motherhood due to a conflict between choosing a private (maternal) and a public (political) womanhood. McAdam (1989) also notes that, when they married, former activists chose partners who espoused similar political views and social commitments and that the high rate of marital separations may have been due to differences in political views.

Second, the younger women in this study clearly perceived that their educational and work histories and those of their male counterparts were adversely affected by movement participation. Although research supports these perceptions in a general sense, some of the findings are contradictory. For example, participants in Argentinean underground movements "explained the interruption of their studies through their participation in armed struggle" (Moyano 1992: 112). In contrast, in U.S. studies, former activists typically achieved significantly higher education than their non-activist counterparts (Marwell et al. 1993). Notwithstanding the apparent contradictions, numerous U.S. studies attest that former activists generally start their careers later, make less money and work less consistently than non-activists (Klandermans 1997; Marwell et al. 1993; McAdam 1989; Van Dyke et al. 2000). However, when gender is considered, the effect of movement participation on these indicators appears reversed for women, possibly due to the impact of second-wave feminism in the United States (Van Dyke et al. 2000).

Third, as I also found, there is a consensus across U.S. studies that former activists have "concentrated in the teaching or other 'helping professions'" (McAdam

1989: 746). Marwell (1993) found that the most common jobs were law, social work and teaching. Nearly half of the respondents in McAdam's (1989) study of Freedom Summer participants expressed strong agreement that participation in social movements had affected their employment choices.

Echoing the experience of the young activists in Arica, McAdam (1989) concluded that the "work and marital histories [of activists] appear to have been shaped, to a remarkable degree, by their politics" (758).

Emotions and Trauma

To say that the experiences shared by las jóvenes were emotionally intense is surely an understatement. Their emotions swung from the exhilaration of adventure and invincibility to the terror of the known and the unknown, from the passion of commitment to the disillusionment of reality. The women experienced untold levels of anger, love, fear, pain, anguish, hope, deception and suspicion.

The emotional aspects of social movement learning are rarely considered. As feminists have long pointed out "patriarchy... has prevented us from making the bridges between our emotional experiences and social conditions which once connected contain the seeds of revolutionary change" (Thompson 1983: 16). The feminist axiom — "the personal is political" — necessarily implies that personal, subjective experience is politically valid knowledge. Jagger (1996) discusses the relationship of emotion to epistemology and Allman (2001a) speculates that "consciousness... also involves our subjective, or emotional, responses" (165). Goodwin, Jasper and Polletta (2001) contend that "emotions are important in all phases of political action, by all types of political actors, across a variety of institutional areas" (16). Recent social movement theorizing suggests that the "explanatory variables" of the current theories are inaccurate or incomplete without the addition of complex emotional realities (Goodwin et al. 2001; Polletta and Amenta 2001).[2]

In dangerous situations, managing fear is essential to survival and to activism. "When protest is extremely risky or dangerous, fear may inhibit collective action (or certain forms of collective action), and so it must be suppressed or at least mitigated, not necessarily in purposive or self-conscious ways, if such action is to occur at all" (Goodwin and Pfaff 2001: 284). The younger activists in Arica demonstrated the same fear management mechanisms as those described by Goodwin and Pfaff, such as intimate social networks, communal gatherings and strong movement identification.

The younger women deeply valued profound friendships, connectedness and solidarity. In a variety of underground organizations, "friendship and political ties were intertwined," observes della Porta (1992a: 8). This has been observed in other women's movements as well. In the U.S. women's movement, for example, "personal ties of love and friendship among members were an important cultural ideal. A willingness to shape personal relationships around the cause was, in large measure, what made possible the intense commitment of members" (Taylor 1989: 769). As can be surmised from the younger women's narratives, movement solidarity is especially important in clandestine or underground movements that depend on secrecy and intense relational ties and that generate high levels of emotion. These can lead to an intense and exclusive collective identity that increasingly insulates and isolates activists from other people and perspectives (della Porta 1992a). DeVries (1996) reasons that this comes "at a cost" (400): The more strongly identified the participant, the deeper the sense of loss and trauma when movement solidarity declines. Thus, to understand the sadness and nostalgia expressed by *las jóvenes* also requires an exploration of their palpable and lingering grief.

"Emotions help to explain not only the origin and spread of social movements but also their decline" (Goodwin et al. 2001: 21). Activists commonly experience exhaustion, frustration and disappointment (Goodwin et al. 2001). When hard-fought struggles lead nowhere or to only partially fulfilled expectations, movement experience "can generate negative, profoundly disempowering learning ... [I]n struggle, workers can learn defeatism, withdrawal and passivity" (Foley 1999: 142).

Many of the consequences experienced by *las jóvenes* might be described in terms of post-traumatic stress disorder (PTSD). While this psychiatric diagnosis cannot be explored in any depth within the confines of a book on learning in social movements, the social-psychological aspects of PTSD provide a window to understanding the consequences experienced by the women. Because of the popular media, we tend to think of PTSD as affecting individuals through nightmares or flashbacks and defence mechanisms such as avoiding, numbing or hypervigilance (van der Kolk and McFarlane 1996). However, deVries (1996) argues that trauma impacts a range of "biological, psychological, social, and cultural phenomena" (400). Furthermore, when viewed from a cultural perspective, trauma "profoundly alters the basic structure not just of the individual, but of the cultural system as a whole: Society will never be the same again" (401). In many situations, a traumatic event or upheaval is buffered by cultural rituals, support systems, historical context and shared identities, according to deVries, and alternative organizational forms can take the place of the lost culture but are often built upon the base of what came before. However, when culture itself has been eviscerated, as in the Chilean situation, where there was a brutal and systematic erasure of the cultural past, the ramifications are tragically far-reaching.

> When cultural protection and security fail, the individual's problems are proportional to the cultural disintegration. The avenues of vulnerability resulting from trauma follow the routes vacated by culture: Paranoia substitutes for trust; aggression replaces nurturance and support; identity confusion or a negative identity substitutes for a positive identity... Compounding these problems in most areas of the world is that at times of cultural disintegration, the population is often physically depleted and fatigued as well.... These psychological and physical consequences will strongly affect their lifestyle and mental state in the future. (408)

Parallels to the Chilean situation are obvious. In order to eradicate any vestiges of Chile's longstanding social democratic tradition, the military government destroyed social organizations, educational materials and cultural traditions. "The dictatorship has outlawed history and so perverted language that Chile's 150 years of democratic tradition are clouded in a fog of unreality" (Villagran 1988: 14). The simplest transgression, such as possessing music by Chile's beloved folk singer Victor Jara, uttering banned words (such as bread or justice) or meeting in groups, was severely punished.

Not surprisingly, the years of terror coupled with years of gruelling and dangerous clandestine struggle took an emotional and physical toll on the women. For the younger women, added to the effects on identity and lifestyle that have already been addressed, are more harmful consequences such as illness, depression or addictions. This came out strongly in the study conducted by Cortez Díaz and Villagra Parra in Arica (1999): "Many women… realized that their poor health was manifested through the body and symbolized psychological and social damage" (130). In the case of Italian, German and Argentinean underground movements, the societal violence perpetrated by the governments germinated a tolerance for violence that was carried into the underground (della Porta 1992b; Moyano 1992; Passerini 1992). Would it be surprising if this were carried into daily life outside the movements? When experienced widely in the society, these deleterious consequences contribute to further erosion of the cultural base, making it increasingly difficult to rebound, much less rebuild.

Finding Hope

In this chapter, I have explored various avenues for understanding the understudied consequences of social movement participation as they apply to learning. But what makes this story so compelling for an adult educator? What does an understanding of social movement consequences contribute to the overall question of learning in social movements? I believe that such deep, traumatic and long-lasting consequences affect the capability and means of learning, unlearning and relearning the self and the society. Re-creating our circumstances and ourselves is an educational process. As one young woman says, "Between finding and losing ourselves, the result is still growth."

During their formative years, *las jóvenes* were informally and contradictorily educated in the streets, learning both repression and resistance. Today, they experience effects in their relationships, their education, their work, their politics and their social world. They are neither politically active nor involved in movements. They have retreated to work with youth and personal development as a way to rebuild and to recover their lost youth and to build the youth of tomorrow. Yet, there is hope in their enduring ties of solidarity, in their commitment to a persistent set of political beliefs and values, in their career commitments and in the pockets of activity that hold their movement in abeyance. In these ways, the women exemplify their previous political commitments in new ways that have an impact on younger generations. The students who make up the new generation of activists are learning from the political consciousness of their elders and are joining them in social movement spaces such as Mujeres de Luto, while at the same time forging their own political identities and spaces in the Penguin Revolution. (See Chovanec and Benitez 2008 for a discussion of intergenerational learning in the student movement.)

Through the process of analyzing the younger women's experience, I came full circle. I originally set out to document the wonderful effects of participating in the women's movement and, instead, was besieged by its detrimental effects. Yet, in reading, re-reading and writing I also discovered glimmers of hope and optimism hidden between the pages of pain and disillusionment. I began to see the women's own words in new ways. My hope is that by exposing the painful and harmful consequences experienced by *las jóvenes* I have created a space to honour and to appreciate the sacrifices they made, not only for themselves, their people and their nation, but also for all of us. I also hope that by highlighting the positive consequences, especially those obscured by their pain and disillusionment, I have opened the possibility for the women in Arica, and for all of us, to see our way to the future.

Perhaps *las jóvenes* are not lost. Perhaps they are a beacon.

Notes

1. Regarding marital status, for example, twenty years after their involvement in Freedom Summer, former participants were less likely to be married than the volunteer applicants who were accepted but who did not show (McAdam 1989). Marwell et al. (1993) found that former U.S. activists were "approximately twice as likely as members of the general college-educated public to be currently divorced or separated" (184). On the subject of parenthood, for example, at age forty, almost half of sixties activists in a U.S. sample were childless (Marwell et al. 1993).

2. For example: social networks necessarily imply affective ties; action is often motivated by injustice frames; collective identity is bounded more by trust, solidarity and affection than by material interests; emotional shifts often accompany cognitive shifts (Goodwin et al. 2001). Especially in high-risk activism with little chance of success, typical analyses of cost-benefit don't apply (Wood 2001).

9

What Is the Role of an Adult Educator in Social Movements?

When we're in the process of mobilizing or organizing it begins to be seen also as an educational problem.... Education is *before*, is *during* and is *after*.... It's impossible to organize without educating and *being* educated by the very process of organizing. (Freire in Horton and Freire 1990: 119–21)

Introduction

Although Freire makes the relationship between education and social movements appear obvious, until recently, social movement scholars have paid little attention to the pedagogical dimension of social movements. The study of the women's movement in Arica, Chile, contributes to an emerging literature that explicitly examines learning and education in social movements. In retracing the women's political lives from before the election of Salvador Allende in 1970, through the Pinochet dictatorship (1973–90), to the present "transition to democracy," the narrative in Part 1 reveals what and how people learn in social movements, including both the processes and the effects that I then explore in Part 2 through the themes of political consciousness, social movement praxis and the consequences of social movement participation. The integral nature of education is underscored in the women's movement in Arica by both its presence (the multiple ways in which the women learned in the women's movement) and its absence (the consequences of the missing "study" or ideological component).

In this final chapter, I present my conclusions about the role of education and adult educators in social movements. I make these claims from within the framework of radical adult education, a form of "adult education theory and practice dedicated to significant social transformation within the left-wing political tradition" (Holst 2002: 4–5). Radical adult education is dedicated to learning that fosters critical revolutionary praxis. As described in Chapter 7, in a critical revolutionary praxis, we "question critically the existing relations and conditions and actively seek to transform or abolish them and to create relations and conditions that will lead to a better future for all human beings" (Allman 2001a: 167–68). However, as Allman (2001b) reasons, "authentic social transformation is never a sudden event. It is a process through which people change not only their circumstances but themselves" (1).

An analysis of the women's movement in Arica provides insight into what that educational "process" might look like in a critical revolutionary praxis. First, learning and education are *organically* integrated into social movements. In other words, learning and education are occurring continuously and spontaneously within social movements. Accordingly, adult educators (whether identified as such or not) are an inherent part of social movements, they are embedded naturally, i.e., organically within the movement. Second, in the process of learning and education in social movements, neither of the two aspects of a critical revolutionary praxis — action and reflection — can be ignored. When a reflective educational dimension is *intentionally and explicitly* integrated into activism, a movement's membership is more effectively mobilized to action, particularly across generations. Third, there are spaces for adult education/educators in the dialectical interaction between the informal organic nature of learning and an intentionally incorporated educational dimension. Three *political-pedagogical* (Freire 2004) *entry points* from which critical revolutionary praxis may be cultivated are the following:

- Adult educators must seize the opportunity to maximize the potentially radical effects of early learning.
- Political parties hold historical promise as institutions of radical adult education.
- Social movement continuity structures offer opportunities for political education in quiescent times.

Organic and Intentional Adult Education

Adult education thus turns out to be the most reliable instrument for social actionists.... Every social action group should at the same time be an adult education group, and I go even so far as to believe that all successful adult education groups sooner or later become social action groups. (Lindeman cited in Rachal 2000: 166)

Lindeman's words underscore the extent of the organic integration of adult education within social movements. Whether intentional or not, learning and education are occurring continuously and spontaneously within social movements.

Learning by persons who are part of a social movement may occur in an informal way because of the stimulation and requirements of participation in a movement... [or] as a result of intentional educational activities organized within the movement itself. Learning for those outside a social movement happens both in informal and intentional ways. The study of social movement learning recognizes that whatever else social movements are or do, they are exceedingly rich learning environments. (Hall and Clover 2005: 584)

Learning politics is an important aspect of the "exceedingly rich learning environment" of social movements identified by Hall and Clover above. Through their material experiences in the women's movement, women in Arica and throughout Latin America recrafted the definition of "political." Of her elders in the women's movement, one young woman observed: "All of them were making ends meet and all of them were organized. And that is political, huh? That is doing politics." In order to "do" politics in a time of economic and political repression, education organically emerged when women needed to learn how to do such things as prepare meals for dozens of people, escape safely from a protest, neutralize the effects of tear gas and make pamphlets. The study group's educational component arose out of the women's own desire to learn more about historical materialism and later, feminism. They believed that an educational, or "study," component integrated with their anti-dictatorship activism would prepare them for "*despúes de*" (after the dictatorship). These kinds of activities exemplify learning *inside* a social movement. When the women orchestrated an event in a supermarket, they were educating others *outside* the movement. Not only did they leave behind the groceries, "we left a symbol as well because not everyone had access to those groceries, only those at some [economic] levels." Similarly, public denunciations and discussion groups in the churches were ways to educate and raise the consciousness of fellow citizens. As these examples illustrate, "The majority of radical adult education ... has occurred in settings not necessarily considered educational, and it has been practiced by people not necessarily considered ... as educators" (Holst 2002: 5). Thus, "adult educators" are embedded naturally within social movements.

Gramsci (1971) had faith in the intellectual and reflective capacities of all citizens. "'Everyone' is a philosopher," he said, "It is not a question of introducing from scratch a scientific form of thought into everyone's individual life, but of renovating and making 'critical' an already existing activity" (330–31). However, he cautions that this does not happen spontaneously. "The active man-in-the-mass [*sic*] has a practical activity but no clear theoretical consciousness of his practical activity" (333). As I pointed out in Chapter 7, activists often concentrate on action while avoiding theory or critical reflection; on the other hand, action often serves as a catalyst for reflection. However, "the real starting place for the political activist is the point that people think" (Allman and Wallis 1995: 125). Everyone thinks, but we may need help to learn to think critically. In Gramsci's view, "organic intellectuals" who arise from within the masses and who remain of the masses, provide such assistance. It is the role of these intellectuals to facilitate the process of critical reflection and analysis.

> There is no organization without intellectuals, that is without organizers and leaders, in other words, without the theoretical aspect of the theory-practice nexus being distinguished concretely by the existence of a people "specialized" in conceptual and philosophical elaboration of ideas. (Gramsci 1971: 334)

This "specialized" person is the organic intellectual. In performing the role of elaborating ideas, the organic intellectual is also an informal adult educator. He or she is a *radical* adult educator when the theory being elaborated is part of a critical revolutionary praxis (see Chapter 7). A young woman was referring to this radical organic dimension when she said: "I began to watch the women leaders ... that were working in the whole women's movement ... We were learning all that they were doing at that time, as the first step ..."

Gramsci also recognized the contribution of traditional intellectuals to social movements. Traditional intellectuals, such as adult educators with scholarly and professional knowledge, who have developed a revolutionary ideology can work effectively together with organic intellectuals. "[Intellectuals] have served as representatives of political science and technology to give the proletariat a consciousness of its historic mission" in order to "construct a proletarian political science" (Gramsci cited in Holst 2002: 109). However, professional and academic adult educators cannot and should not position themselves as outside experts. As with organic intellectuals, only by being "organically" present in social movements, and immersed in the work of the movement, will the disciplinary knowledge and skills of adult educators be useful in a critical revolutionary praxis. As a teacher, one woman exemplified this traditional but organic educational role in an example about the free milk program instituted by the Allende government and thwarted by the contra-Allende faction: "Well, suddenly, we found that the parents were refusing to take the milk ... So, we handed out recipes of how to use the milk in desserts, in this and that, so that the people would take it."

Thus, educational processes are not left entirely to chance in effective social movement organizing. Social movements are more effective when activists and organizers deliberately dedicate attention to the pedagogical dimension of organizing and activism. In particular, in the process of learning and education in social movements, neither of the two aspects of a critical revolutionary praxis can be ignored — neither action, nor reflection.

In Chapter 6, I described the women's steadfast political consciousness, and in Chapter 7, I argued that this was not enough to sustain their activism into the transition period. I proposed that the reflective dimension of critical revolutionary praxis requires the "cement" of ideology to enhance social movement effectiveness and longevity (Allman and Wallis 1997). In the desperation of an oppressive situation, the women in Arica intuitively united across political party lines for a common purpose. Recall the detentions that led to the women's protest at the courthouse and from which "the women's struggle in Arica was born." Even in such a seemingly spontaneous resistance of "disparate social elements," Gramsci recognized the educational role of the leaders, even when a "conscious leadership" is not visible. In his analysis of the Turin movement in 1920, when factory workers collectively seized control of the means of production, Gramsci (1971) observed the congruent relationship among spontaneity, leadership and education.

> This element of "spontaneity" was not neglected and even less despised. It was *educated*, directed, purged of extraneous contaminations; the aim was

to bring it into line with modern theory — but in a living and historically effective manner. The leaders themselves spoke of the "spontaneity" of the movement, and rightly so. This assertion was a stimulus, a tonic, an element of unification in depth; above all it denied that the movement was arbitrary, a cooked-up venture, and stressed its historical necessity. It gave the masses a "theoretical" consciousness of being creators of historical and institutional values, of being founders of a State. This unity between "spontaneity" and "conscious leadership" or "discipline" is precisely the real political action of the subaltern classes, in so far as this is mass politics. (198)

The "modern theory" to which Gramsci refers is theory that provides the tools to analyze and critique the material conditions of capitalism. As I argued in Chapter 7, a critique of capitalism must lie at the heart of a cementing ideology for social movements. In this way, the specific situation of Arica would be inserted into a global framework that considers "transnational power structures," avoiding the common activist pitfall of focusing on a single issue in a local context. Theories of transnationalism look at the "transnational economic links and cultural asymmetries" and the oppositional discourses and practices within them (Grewal and Kaplan 1994: 3). According to Allman (2001b), "We need to develop a critical understanding of how all of these and other issues link together in a total structure, a human structure, of oppression welded together by the social relations and objectives of global capitalism" (6). For feminists, this analysis would include acknowledging "links between transnational power structures" (Grewal and Kaplan 1994: 27) such as the relationship between capitalism and patriarchy. "We know that there is an imperative need to address the concerns of women around the world in the historicized particularity of their relationship to multiple patriarchies as well as to international economic hegemonies" (Grewal and Kaplan 1994: 17).

Understandings about transnational capital, market-driven globalization, liberalization of financial markets, international monetary institutions and all the other machinations of neo-liberalism are much harder to grasp than the specific "enemy" embodied in one unquestionably brutal dictator. Effectively tackling the more amorphous "enemy" requires the roll-up-your-sleeves, soul-searching, uncomfortable, conflictual, collaborative work of dealing with difference and diversity, while at the same time working towards constructing and sustaining solidarity of purpose. The gender discrimination in social and political movements of the left and the class and racial discrimination in the women's movement, among other forms of domination *within* oppositional struggles, are well known. The only way forward is to recognize multiple and intersecting oppressions and contextualize them within broader political, economic and historical issues and interests. As one astute woman leader stated:

To maintain a homogenous movement or to have a common line of thought, [we have] to learn to work through the diversity, respecting the differences — a thing that we don't know how to achieve even in the feminist movement, much less in the other movements.

Applying critical consciousness and analytic capacities to the current material conditions existing in Chile and throughout the world, offers a starting place for a renewed pedagogy of critique and revitalized pedagogy of hope (Lange 2001). An educational process that starts from this new place and builds on the past incorporates a dialogue about "not only what we are doing but also our reflections on why we have chosen to engage in a particular struggle and how we think this might relate to the global campaign for social transformation" (Allman 2001b: 5).

Political-Pedagogical Entry Points

Adult educators must seize the opportunity to maximize the potentially radical effects of early learning.

Parents are clearly implicated in the early political socialization of their children. The learning trajectory of the women activists in Arica reveals the powerful influence of parents as the first political educators of the next generation. In turn, woman activists in Arica became seasoned political educators, dedicated to parenting in ways that promote critical socio-political consciousness. One young mother identifies this intergenerational parenting effect. "You are left with that learning and that learning you transmit to your children as well," she declares.

While all parents transmit basic values to their children and many intentionally educate their children in ethical and critical thinking, how many recognize our role as political educators of our children? How many parents have the skills to nurture our children's journey towards a critical revolutionary praxis? In the North American context, political education is hardly considered in the parenting repertoire, and adult educators have paid little attention to their role in educating parents to be political educators. As a first step, adult educators must be attentive to the pedagogical openings afforded by the early learning experiences of adults. As Lange (2004) discovered:

> Ethics of "honesty, integrity, fairness, courage, respect, loyalty, community service, and citizen responsibility" did not require transformation but restoration to a rightful place in their lives and in society at large. Contrary to various social analyses, these ethics were not missing among these participants but had been submerged. (130)

Within the literature, the emphasis on the transformation of naïve consciousness to critical consciousness (Freire 2003/1973) appears to preclude or ignore the possibility that the original starting place may be less naïve and more critical than initially supposed. I contend that parents are the "organic intellectuals" within family and community social systems and that there is radical pedagogical potential in parenting. Adult educators must find ways to provide political education to parents for this important foundational work.

Political parties hold historical promise as institutions of radical adult education. Most of the women interviewed in Arica were members of political parties that played a significant educational role in the consolidation of their political consciousness. However, while the older women were explicitly educated in the political ideologies of their parties, the younger women decried the failure of their political party elders to provide the ideological education that contributes to the theoretical clarity and critical analysis needed for sustained activism. Although their educational role was marginalized during the dictatorship, political parties in Chile still have considerable influence on the political education of citizens, including on youth, as in the example of the Penguins leader quoted in Chapter 6.

In contrast, Canadian political parties are an undervalued and near-forgotten educational resource. Holst (2002) makes a similar claim about the U.S. context:

> A theory and practice of revolutionary or radical adult education must explore the pedagogical nature of the most widely adopted and successful form of revolutionary organization of the twentieth century. One could make the case that, in the twentieth century, more radical adult education took place in revolutionary parties than in any other forum, yet the literature, with few exceptions... has virtually ignored the educational role of revolutionary parties. (113)

Taking his cue from Gramsci, Holst argues that it is the role of the political party to provide the educational leadership needed for the development of a political consciousness. When political parties assume their role as political "schools," the party is in a position to "elaborate" the organic intellectual from within itself: "Organic intellectuals are not born but are formed through the educational activities of working-class parties" (Holst 2002: 110). This is clearly exemplified by one younger woman who recognized her own development as a leader within the Young Communists:

> I believe that it was in la Jota that I learned to identify myself with a social role... They asked my opinion in the meeting. I was nervous, my hands sweated, and my stomach turned like this. We were in a meeting and I had to speak. If a *compañero* reads a political tract, you have to analyze it. So, I was learning like that, right from how one develops as a person. Also, in acquiring roles, the *compañera* can be the head of the organization.

Freire (2004) argues that "the pedagogical-political position of progressive parties should be to insist on an analysis" (114). From Freire and Gramsci, Allman (2001b) illuminates the methodology inherent in this pedagogical project. She particularly emphasizes the mutuality of the teacher/learner relationship and dismisses any idea that the "elite" core of organic or traditional intellectuals would be dogmatic or directive. According to Freire, she states, "their role is not to tell the people what to think but to enable them also to think critically. His contribution is an analysis of how to be *with* the people so they can develop this way of thinking" (90). From Gramsci, she recounts: "The leader's or radical educator's role is to persuade and encourage people to undertake these renovations and to help them question their already existing activity (common-sense thinking) until it becomes 'critical' activity (dialectical thinking)" (115).

Resurrected to their historical place in society, revitalized for the current realities of transnational capital and purged of the sexism and other oppressive apparatuses that have infiltrated most "progressive" or "revolutionary" institutions, political parties hold historical promise as institutions of radical adult education.

Social movement continuity structures offer opportunities for political education in quiescent times.
In analyzing the women's movement in Chile over the past century, from suffrage and workers' struggles in the early part of the century to anti-dictatorship activism in the 1980s to the student movement today, threads of continuity appear. In their account of the grassroots women's movement in Chile, Valdés and Weinstein (1993) explicitly note the continuity between two historical expressions of the movement.

> Once the right to vote was obtained, the particular struggle of women to change their subordinate position in society diminished in its presence and vitality. However, the participation of women in popular mobilizations that pressured for an improved quality of life continued to be important, "*tomas de terreno*" [land takeovers] stands out, where women were the protagonists many times. (48)

As I noted in Chapter 8, personal development, motherwork, career work and the persistent presence of the feminist NGO, CEDEMU, as well as the annual event, Mujeres de Luto, are examples of social movement continuity structures in Arica today. In terms of intergenerational learning in social movements, the political consciousness of the earlier generations as manifested in both their day-to-day routines and through public activities has perhaps contributed to the mobilization of the Penguins student movement today (Chovanec and Benitez 2008). In 2006, the women recognized this dynamic in relation to the growing presence of the younger generation at Mujeres de Luto:

> It has something to do also with the way we have raised consciousness in the family and in friends and in the political and social arena because now women have become sympathetic to us and joined, that in past would just watch us walk by… That is the objective of us who have been standing there year after year, to inculcate in the youth —our friends and our children — to continue… even after we are gone.

Between the "waves" of women's or other social movements is a period in which "individuals and groups continue the struggle at the grassroots in workplaces, within other social movements, and in the rhythms of daily life" (Whittier 1995: 21). Freire (2004) also perceives the significance of this micro level activity:

> The ideological, political, pedagogical, and ethical fight put up by those who position themselves in line with a progressive option chooses no particular time or place. It takes place at home, in relations between fathers, mothers, sons, and daughters as well as in school, at any level, and within work relationships. (33)

Social movement researchers further speculate that a cadre of highly committed activists with a rich political and ideological culture keep the movement in a holding pattern that contributes to later mobilization through "preexisting activist networks, a repertoire of goals and tactics, and a collective identity" (Taylor 1989: 770). Klandermans (1997) suggests that established activist networks increase the likelihood of subsequent activism through a "spiral of commitment and participation" (111). Taylor concludes, "Movements do not die, but scale down and retrench" (772). From CEDEMU's perspective, "the little influence that the women's movement has is through a small movement, and achievements [are made] because there are groups of very committed women that move things."

Social movements survive in the visceral complexities of people's personal lives and in the public spaces nurtured across generations. In these enduring spaces — of memory, activity and possibility — exist insistent opportunities for adult educators to facilitate meaningful reflective activity. These are educational spaces for the foundational work of consciousness-raising, critical analysis and visioning that provides the ideological grounding for social movements. They are spaces that celebrate the past, cultivate participation in the present and prefigure the future. It is our task to find and nurture these spaces in our own lives and social contexts in order to extend the political-pedagogical mission of social movements.

Final Word

Radical adult education occurs through the organic presence of adult educators within social movements in a dialectical relationship with organizing. Even informal learning is more effective if intentionally nurtured across generations. I propose that social movements deliberately incorporate an educational dimension to ensure intergenerational political learning. Parents, political parties and social movement continuity structures are political-pedagogical entry points for the kind of political socialization and education needed to revitalize and mobilize social movements over time. Paulo Freire and Miles Horton encourage adult educators to work in just these kinds of spaces:

> Both agree that even "little pockets of hope and adventurism" can provide the context of education for social change... However, they also agree that these small pockets can no more be created at will than can larger

revolutionary situations. In generally quiescent times the challenge for progressive adult educators is not to initiate abstract general educational campaigns so much as to find and foster and serve these "pockets of hope." This, they stress, is "not an intellectual process (but) a process of being involved." (Miles 1996: 277)

"A process of being involved" — this is precisely what I learned from the women's movement in Arica about how to be an adult educator in a social movement. Thus, the question is not what is the role of an adult educator in social movements? Rather, the more appropriate question is *what is the role of the social movement in the adult educator?*

References

Agar, Michael H. 1980. *The Professional Stranger: An Informal Introduction to Ethnography*. San Diego: Academic Press.

Agosín, Marjorie. 1996. *Tapestries of Hope, Threads of Love: The Arpillera Movement in Chile, 1974–1994*. Translated by Celeste Kostopulos-Cooperman. Albuquerque, NM: University of New Mexico Press.

Alarcón Ferrari, Cristián. 2007. "The Student Movement in Chile during 2006 and Beyond: Reclaiming the Right to Education in a Worldwide Symbol of Free Market, Neo-Liberalism and Capitalist Hegemony." Proceedings of the fifth Critical Management Studies Conference, University of Manchester, Manchester, UK.

Allman, Paula. 2001a. *Critical Education against Global Capitalism*. Westport, CT: Bergin and Garvey.

———. 2001b. *Revolutionary Social Transformation: Democratic Hopes, Political Possibilities, and Critical Education, Critical Studies in Education and Culture*. Westport, CT: Bergin & Garvey.

Allman, Paula, and John Wallis. 1995. "Gramsci's Challenge to the Politics of the Left in 'Our Times.'" *International Journal of Lifelong Education* 14, 2.

———. 1997. "Commentary: Paulo Freire and the Future of the Radical Tradition." *Studies in the Education of Adults* 29, 2.

Allman, Paula, and Paul Wallis. 1988. "Karl Marx's Theoretical Contributions to Radical Adult Education." In M. Zukas (ed.), *Papers from the Transatlantic Dialogue, University of Leeds, July 11–13, 1988*. Leeds: School of Continuing Education.

Alvarez, Sonia E. 1990. *Engendering Democracy in Brazil: Women's Movements in Transition Politics*. Princeton, NJ: Princeton University Press.

Baldez, Lisa. 2002. *Why Women Protest: Women's Movements in Chile*. Cambridge, UK: Cambridge University Press.

Bannerji, Himani. 1995. *Thinking Through: Essays on Feminism, Marxism, and Anti-Racism*. Toronto: Women's Press.

Berman, Sheldon. 1997. *Children's Social Consciousness and the Development of Social Responsibility*. New York: SUNY Press.

Bevington, Douglas, and Chris Dixon. 2005. "Movement-Relevant Theory: Rethinking Social Movement Scholarship and Activism." *Social Movement Studies* 4, 3.

Braungart, Richard G., and Margaret M. Braungart. 1993. "Historical Generations and Citizenship: 200 Years of Youth Movements." In Philo C. Wasburn (ed.), *Research in Political Sociology*. Greenwich, CT: JAI Press.

Bresnahan, Rosalind. 2003. "Introduction: Chile Since 1990: The Contradictions of Neoliberal Democratization." *Latin American Perspectives* 30, 5.

Brookfield, Stephen D. 2000. "Transformative Learning as Ideology Critique." In Jack Mezirow and Associates (ed.), *Learning as Transformation: Critical Perspectives on a Theory in Progress*. San Fransisco: Jossey-Bass.

Carroll, William K. 1997. "Social Movements and Counterhegemony: Canadian Contexts and Social Theories." In William K. Carroll (ed.), *Organizing Dissent: Contemporary Social Movements in Theory and Practice*. Second edition. Toronto: Garamond Press.

Chaney, Elsa M. 1974. "The Mobilization of Women in Allende's Chile." In Jane Jaquette (ed.), *Women in Politics*. New York: John Wiley and Sons.

Chavkin, Samuel. 1985. *Storm over Chile: The Junta under Siege*. Westport, CT: Lawrence Hill and Company.

Chinchilla, Norma Stolz. 1992. "Marxism, Feminism, and the Struggle for Democracy in Latin America." In Arturo Escobar and Sonia E. Alvarez (eds.), *The Making of Social Movements in Latin America: Identity, Strategy, and Democracy*. Boulder, CO: Westview Press.

Chovanec, Donna M. 1994. "The Experience of Consciousness-Raising in Abused Women." MEd thesis, Adult, Career and Technology Education, University of Alberta, Edmonton, AB.

_____. 2004. "Between Hope and Despair: Social and Political Learning in the Women's Movement in Chile." PhD thesis, Educational Policy Studies, University of Alberta, Edmonton, AB.

Chovanec, Donna M., and Alexandra Benitez. 2008. "The Penguin Revolution in Chile: Exploring Intergenerational Learning in Social Movements." *Journal of Contemporary Issue in Education* 3, 1.

Chovanec, Donna M., Sandra Bravo and Héctor González. 2002. "Libreto: El Aprendizaje Del Poder Desde Los Margenes: Movimientos Populares De Mujeres En Chile." Unpublished manuscript, Arica, Chile.

Chuchryk, Patricia M. 1989. "Feminist Anti-Authoritarian Politics: The Role of Women's Organizations in the Chilean Transition to Democracy." In Jane S. Jaquette (ed.), *The Women's Movement in Latin America: Feminism and the Transition to Democracy*. Boston: Unwin Hyman.

Cohen, Jean L. 1985. "Strategy or Identity: New Theoretical Paradigms and Contemporary Social Movements." *Social Research* 52, 4.

Collard, Sue, and Michael Law. 1989. "The Limits of Perspective Transformation: A Critique of Mezirow's Theory." *Adult Education Quarterly* 39, 2.

Collins, Michael. 1991. *Adult Education as Vocation: A Critical Role for the Adult Educator*. New York: Routledge.

Cook, Judith A., and Mary Margaret Fonow. 1990. "Knowledge and Women's Interests: Issues of Epistemology and Methodology in Feminist Sociological Research." In Joyce McCarl Nielsen (ed.), *Feminist Research Methods: Exemplary Readings in the Social Sciences*. Boulder, CO: Westview Press.

Cortez Díaz, Aylen, and Milka Villagra Parra. 1999. "Imaginario y Prácticas Socio-Políticas de las Mujeres Opositoras a la Dictadura Militar en Chile." Unpublished manuscript, Arica, Chile.

Coulson, Margaret A., and Carol Riddell. 1980. *Approaching Sociology*. London: Routledge and Kegan Paul.

Craske, Nikki. 1998. "Remasculinisation and the Neoliberal State in Latin America." In V. Randall and G. Waylen (eds.), *Gender, Politics and the State*. London: Routledge.

Croteau, David, William Hoynes and Charlotte Ryan (eds.). 2005. *Rhyming Hope and History: Activists, Academics, and Social Movement Scholarship*. Minneapolis: University of Minnesota Press.

Cunningham, Phyllis M. 1992. "From Freire to Feminism: The North American Experience with Critical Pedagogy." *Adult Education Quarterly* 42, 3.

della Porta, Donatella. 1992a. "Introduction: On Individual Motivations in Underground Political Organizations." *International Social Movement Research* 4.

_____. 1992b. "Political Socialization in Left Wing Underground Organizations." *International Social Movement Research* 4.

della Porta, Donatella, and Mario Diani. 2006. *Social Movements: An Introduction.* Second edition. Malden, MA: Blackwell Publishing.

deVries, Marten W. 1996. "Trauma in Cultural Perspective." In Bessel A. van der Kolk, Alexander C. McFarlane and Lars Weisaeth (eds.), *Traumatic Stress: The Effects of Overwhelming Experience on Mind, Body, and Society.* New York: Guilford Press.

Dykstra, Corina, and Michael Law. 1994. "Popular Social Movements as Educative Forces: Towards a Theoretical Framework." Proceedings of the 35th Adult Education Research Conference, University of Tennessee, Knoxville, TN.

Equipo de Educación Popular. n.d. *El Juego del Siglo: Episodios de la Historia del Pueblo de Chile.* Santiago, Chile: CIDE.

Escobar, Arturo. 1992. "Culture, Economics, and Politics in Latin American Social Movements: Theory and Research." In Arturo Escobar and Sonia E. Alvarez (eds.), *The Making of Social Movements in Latin America.* Boulder, CO: Westview Press.

Escobar, Arturo, and Sonia E. Alvarez. 1992. "Introduction: Theory and Protest in Latin America Today." In Arturo Escobar and Sonia E. Alvarez (eds.), *The Making of Social Movements in Latin America: Identity, Strategy, and Democracy.* Boulder, CO: Westview Press.

Finger, Matthias. 1989. "New Social Movements and Their Implications for Adult Education." *Adult Education Quarterly* 40, 1.

Foley, Griff. 1999. *Learning in Social Action: A Contribution to Understanding Informal Education.* London: Zed Books.

Frampton, Caelie, Gary Kinsman, A.K. Thompson and Kate Tilleczek (eds.). 2006. *Sociology for Changing the World: Social Movements/Social Research.* Halifax, NS: Fernwood Publishing.

Franceschet, Susan. 2001. "Women in Politics in Post-Transitional Democracies: The Chilean Case." *International Feminist Journal of Politics* 3, 2.

_____. 2003. "State Feminism" and Women's Movements: The Impact of Chile's Servicio Nacional de la Mujer on Women's Activism." *Latin American Research Review* 38, 1.

_____. 2005. *Women and Politics in Chile.* Boulder, CO: Lynne Rienner.

Freire, Paulo. 2002. *Education for Critical Consciousness.* New York: Continuum.

_____. 2003/1973. *Pedagogy of the Oppressed.* Translated by Myra Bergman Ramos. New York: Continuum.

_____. 2004. *Pedagogy of Indignation.* Boulder, CO: Paradigm.

Gaviola, Edda, Eliana Largo and Sandra Palestro. 1994. *Una Historia Necessaria: Mujeres En Chile 1973–1990.* Santiago, Chile: Authors.

González, Héctor M. 1997. "Conciencia Socialista and Education in Cuba." MEd thesis, Educational Policy Studies, University of Alberta, Edmonton, AB.

Goodwin, Jeff, James M. Jasper and Francesca Polletta. 2001. "Introduction: Why Emotions Matter." In Jeff Goodwin, James M. Jasper and Francesca Polletta (eds.), *Passionate Politics: Emotions and Social Movements.* Chicago: University of Chicago Press.

Goodwin, Jeff, and Steven Pfaff. 2001. "Emotion Work in High-Risk Social Movements: Managing Fear in the U.S. and East German Civil Rights Movement." In Jeff Goodwin, James M. Jasper and Francesca Polletta (eds.), *Passionate Politics: Emotions and Social Movements.* Chicago: University of Chicago Press.

Gouin, Rachel. 2009. "An Antiracist Feminist Analysis for the Study of Learning in Social

Struggle." *Adult Education Quarterly* 59, 2 .

Gramsci, Antonio. 1971. *Selections from the Prison Notebooks.* Translated by Quinton Hoare and Geoffrey Nowell Smith. New York: International Publishers.

Grewal, Inderpal, and Karen Kaplan. 1994. "Introduction: Transnational Feminist Practices and Questions of Postmodernity." In Inderpal Grewal and Karen Kaplan (eds.), *Scattered Hegemonies: Postmodernity and Transnational Feminist Practices.* Minneapolis: University of Minnesota Press.

Hall, Budd L. 2006. "Social Movement Learning: Theorizing a Canadian Tradition." In Tara Fenwick, Tom Nesbit and Bruce Spencer (eds.), *Contexts of Adult Education: Canadian Perspectives.* Toronto: Thompson Educational Publishing.

Hall, Budd L., and Darlene Clover. 2005. "Social Movement Learning." In L.M. English (ed.), *International Encyclopaedia of Adult Education.* New York: Palgrave.

Hall, Budd L., Darlene E. Clover, Winnie Chow, Odette Laramee and Ellie Langford Parks. 2006. "Social Movement Learning and the Arts in Adult Education: Reports on the State of the Field." Proceedings of the L'Association Canadienne pour l'Étude de l'Éducation des Adultes (ACÉÉA)/Canadian Association for the Study of Adult Education (CASAE) 2006 National Conference York University. Toronto, ON.

Hall, Budd, and Thomas Turay. 2006. "State of the Field Report: Social Movement Learning." Vancouver, BC: University of British Columbia.

Hart, Mechtild U. 1990. "Liberation through Consciousness Raising." In J. Mezirow and Associates (eds.), *Fostering Critical Reflection in Adulthood: A Guide to Transformative and Emancipatory Learning.* San Fransisco: Jossey Bass.

Hartsock, Nancy C.M. 1983. "The Feminist Standpoint: Developing the Ground for a Specifically Feminist Historical Materialism." In Sandra Harding and Merrill Hintikka (eds.), *Discovering Reality.* London: D. Reidl.

Hellman, Judith Adler. 1992. "The Study of New Social Movements in Latin America and the Question of Autonomy." In Arturo Escobar and Sonia E. Alvarez (eds.), *The Making of Social Movements in Latin America.* Boulder, CO: Westview Press.

Hipsher, Patricia L. 1996. "Democratization and the Decline of Urban Social Movements in Chile and Spain." *Comparative Politics* 28, 3.

Holford, John. 1995. "Why Social Movements Matter: Adult Education Theory, Cognitive Praxis, and the Creation of Knowledge." *Adult Education Quarterly* 45, 2.

Holst, John D. 2002. *Social Movements, Civil Society, and Radical Adult Education.* Westport, CT: Bergin and Garvey.

Horton, Myles, and Paulo Freire. 1990. *We Make the Road by Walking: Conversations on Education and Social Change.* Philadelphia, MA: Temple University Press.

Internationalist Striker. 2006. "March of the Penguins: Chile Students Arise." June 13. Available at <http://www.melbourne.indymedia.org/news/2006/06/114659.php> (accessed on March 28, 2007).

Jaggar, Alison M. 1996. "Love and Knowledge: Emotion in Feminist Epistemology." In Ann Garry and Marilyn Pearsall (eds.), *Women, Knowledge, and Reality: Explorations in Feminist Philosophy.* New York: Routledge.

Jaquette, Jane S. 1989. "Conclusion: Women and the New Democratic Politics." In Jane S. Jaquette (ed.), *The Women's Movement in Latin America: Feminism and the Transition to Democracy.* Boston: Unwin Hyman.

Jelin, Elizabeth. 1990. "Citizenship and Identity: Final Reflections." In Elizabeth Jelin (ed.), *Women and Social Change in Latin America.* London: Zed Books and United Nations

References

Research Institute for Social Development.

Kastner, Andrea. 1993. "Knowledge and Curriculum in Contemporary Social Movements." Proceedings of the 34th Annual Adult Education Research Conference, University Park, PA.

Kilgore, Deborah W. 1999. "Understanding Learning in Social Movements: A Theory of Collective Learning." *International Journal of Lifelong Education* 18, 3.

Kirkwood, Julieta. 1986. *Ser Política en Chile: Las Feministas y Los Partidos*. Santiago, Chile: FLACSO.

Klandermans, Bert. 1997. *The Social Psychology of Protest*. Cambridge, MA: Blackwell.

Lange, Elizabeth Ann. 2001. "Living Transformation: Beyond Midlife Crisis to Restoring Ethical Space." PhD thesis, Educational Policy Studies, University of Alberta, Edmonton, AB.

_____. 2004. "Transformative and Restorative Learning: A Vital Dialectic for Sustainable Societies." *Adult Education Quarterly* 54, 2.

MacKinnon, Catharine. 1997. "Feminism, Marxism, Method, and the State: An Agenda for Theory." In Diana Tietjens Meyers (ed.), *Feminist Social Thought: A Reader*. New York: Routledge.

Mahrousse, Gada. 2008. "Race-Conscious Transnational Activists with Cameras: Mediators of Compassion." *International Journal of Cultural Studies* 11, 1.

Marwell, Gerald, Michael T. Aiken and N.J. Demerath III. 1987. "The Persistence of Political Attitudes among 1960s Civil Rights Activists." *Public Opinion Quarterly* 51.

Marwell, Gerald, N.J. Demerath III, and Michael T. Aiken. 1993. "1960s Civil Rights Activists Turn Forty: A Generational Unit at Mid-Life." In Philo C. Wasburn (ed.), *Research in Political Sociology*. Greenwich, CT: JAI Press.

Marx, Gary T., and Douglas McAdam. 1994. *Collective Behavior and Social Movements: Process and Structure*. Englewood Cliffs, NJ: Prentice Hall.

McAdam, Doug. 1989. "The Biographical Consequences of Activism." *American Sociological Review* 54.

_____. 1992. "Gender as a Mediator of the Activist Experience: The Case of Freedom Summer." *American Journal of Sociology* 97, 5.

McLellan, David (ed.). 1977. *Karl Marx: Selected Writings*. Oxford, UK: Oxford University Press.

Mezirow, Jack. 2000. "Learning to Think Like an Adult: Core Concepts of Transformation Theory." In Jack Mezirow and Associates (ed.), *Learning as Transformation: Critical Perspectives on a Theory in Progress*. San Fransisco: Jossey-Bass.

Mezirow, Jack, and Associates (eds.). 1990. *Fostering Critical Reflection in Adulthood*. San Fransisco: Jossey Bass.

Miles, Angela. 1996. "Adult Education for Global Social Change: Feminism and Women's Movement." In Paul Wangoola and Frank Youngman (eds.), *Towards a Transformative Political Economy of Adult Education*. DeKalb, IL: LEPS Press.

Miller, Francesca. 1990. "Latin American Feminism and the Transnational Arena." In Emilie Bergman, Janet Greenberg, Gwen Kirkpatrick, Francine Masiello, Francesca Miller, Marta Morello-Frosch, Kathleen Newman and Mary Louise Pratt (eds.), *Women, Culture, and Politics in Latin America: Seminar on Feminism and Culture in Latin America*. Berkeley, CA: University of California Press.

_____. 1995. "Latin American Women and the Search for Social, Political, and Economic Transformation." In Sandor Halebsky and Richard L. Harris (eds.), *Capital, Power, and*

Inequality in Latin America. Boulder, CO: Westview Press.

Mohanty, Chandra Talpade. 1991. "Cartographies of Struggle: Third World Women and the Politics of Feminism." In Chandra Talpade Mohanty, Ann Russo and Lourdes Torres (eds.), *Third World Women and the Politics of Feminism*. Bloomington, IL: Indiana University Press.

_____. 2003. *Feminism without Borders: Decolonizing Theory, Practicing Solidarity*. Durham and London: Duke University Press.

Montecino, Sonia. 1996. *Madres y Huachos: Alegorías del Mestizaje Chileno*. Santiago, Chile: Editorial Sudamericana.

Morrow, Raymond A., and Carlos Alberto Torres. 2002. *Reading Freire and Habermas: Critical Pedagogy and Transformative Social Change*. New York: Teacher's College Press.

Moyano, Maria Jose. 1992. "Going Underground in Argentina: A Look at the Founders of a Guerilla Movement." *International Social Movement Research* 4.

Noonan, Rita K. 1995. "Women against the State: Political Opportunities and Collective Action Frames in Chile's Transition to Democracy." *Sociological Forum* 10, 1.

Okeke-Ihejirika, E., and Susan Franceschet. 2002. "Democratization and State Feminism: Gender Politics in Africa and Latin America." *Development and Change* 33, 3.

Olavarría, Margot. 2003. "Protected Neoliberalism: Perverse Institutionalization and the Crisis of Representation in Postdictatorship Chile." *Latin American Perspectives* 30, 6.

Parrish, Marilyn McKinley, and Edward W. Taylor. 2007. "Seeking Authenticity: Women and Learning in the Catholic Worker Movement." *Adult Education Quarterly* 57, 3.

Passerini, Luisa. 1992. "Lacerations in the Memory: Women in the Italian Underground Organizations." *International Social Movement Research* 4.

Polletta, Francesca, and Edwin Amenta. 2001. "Second That Emotion? Lessons from Once-Novel Concepts in Social Movement Research." In Jeff Goodwin, James M. Jasper and Francesca Polletta (eds.), *Passionate Politics: Emotions and Social Movements*. Chicago: University of Chicago Press.

Quiroz Martin, Teresa. 1997. "Women, Poverty and Adult Education in Chile." In Shirley Walters (ed.), *Globalization, Adult Education and Training: Impacts and Issues*. London: Zed Books.

Rachal, John R. 2000. "We'll Never Turn Back: Adult Education and the Struggle for Citizenship in Mississippi's Freedom Summer." *Adult Education Quarterly* 50, 3.

Razack, Sherene. 2007. "Stealing the Pain of Others: Reflections on Canadian Humanitarian Responses." *Review of Education, Pedagogy and Cultural Studies* 29, 4.

Rojas, Luis Emilio. n.d. *Nueva y Moderna Historia de Chile*. Santiago, Chile: Gong.

Ryan, Charlotte. 2005. "Successful Collaboration: Movement Building in the Media Arena." In David Croteau, William Hoynes and Charlotte Ryan (eds.), *Rhyming Hope and History: Activists, Academics, and Social Movement Scholarship*. Minneapolis: University of Minnesota Press.

Schild, Verónica. 1991. "Gender, Class and Politics: Poor Neighbourhood Organizing in Authoritarian Chile." PhD thesis, Political Science, University of Toronto, Toronto, ON.

_____. 1994. "Recasting 'Popular' Movements: Gender and Political Learning in Neighborhood Organizations in Chile." *Latin American Perspectives* 21, 2.

_____. 1998. "New Subjects of Rights? Women's Movements and the Construction of

Citizenship in The 'New Democracies.'" In Sonia E. Alvarez, Evelina Dagnino and Arturo Escobar (eds.), *Cultures of Politics, Politics of Cultures: Re-Visioning Latin American Social Movements*. Boulder, CO: Westview Press.

_____. 2000. "Gender Equality" without Social Justice: Women's Rights in the Neoliberal Age. NACLA *Report on the Americas*, 25–28.

Schuurman, Frans J. 1993. "Modernity, Post-Modernity and the New Social Movements." In Frans J. Schuurman (ed.), *Beyond the Impasse: New Directions in Development Theory*. London: Zed Books.

Scott, Sue M. 2003. "The Social Construction of Transformation." *Journal of Transformative Education* 1, 3.

Se Encadenó Esposa De Dirigente Preso. 1988. *La Estrella*. July 18, 7.

Silva, Eduardo. 1991. "The Political Economy of Chile's Regime Transition: From Radical to 'Pragmatic' Neo-Liberal Policies." In Paul W. Drake and Iván Jaksic (eds.), *The Struggle for Democracy in Chile, 1982–1990*. Lincoln, NE: University of Nebraska Press.

Snow, David A., and Catherine Corrigall-Brown. 2005. "Falling on Deaf Ears: Confronting the Prospect of Non-Resonant Frames." In David Croteau, William Hoynes and Charlotte Ryan (eds.), *Rhyming Hope and History: Activists, Academics, and Social Movement Scholarship*. Minneapolis: University of Minnesota Press.

Spencer, Bruce. 1998. *The Purposes of Adult Education: A Guide for Students*. Toronto: Thompson Educational Publishing.

Spradley, James P. 1980. *Participant Observation*. New York: Harcourt Brace Jovanovich.

Taylor, Verta. 1989. "Social Movement Continuity: The Women's Movement in Abeyance." *American Sociological Review* 54, October.

Thompson, A.K. 2006. "Direct Action: Pedagogy of the Oppressed." In Caelie Frampton, Gary Kinsman, A.K. Thompson and Kate Tilleczek (eds.), *Sociology for Changing the World: Social Movements/Social Research*. Halifax, NS: Fernwood Publishing.

Thompson, Jane. 1983. *Learning Liberation: Women's Response to Men's Education — Radical Forum on Adult Education*. London: Croom Helm.

Universidad de Chile. 1972. *Enciclopedia de Arica*. Arica, Chile: Author.

Valdés, Teresa, and Marisa Weinstein. 1993. *Mujeres que Sueñan: Las Organizaciones de Pobladoras en Chile, 1973–1999*. Santiago, Chile: FLACSO-Chile.

van der Kolk, Bessel A., and Alexander C. McFarlane. 1996. "The Black Hole of Trauma." In Bessel A. van der Kolk, Alexander C. McFarlane and Lars Weisaeth (eds.), *Traumatic Stress: The Effects of Ovewhelming Experience on Mind, Body, and Society*. New York: Guilford Press.

Van Dyke, Nell, Doug McAdam and Brenda Wilhelm. 2000. "Gendered Outcomes: Gender Differences in the Biographical Consequences of Activism." *Mobilization: An International Journal* 5, 2.

van Manen, Max. 1990. *Researching Lived Experience: Human Science for an Action Sensitive Pedagogy*. London, ON: Althouse Press.

Villagran, Fernando. 1988. "Me or Chaos." *Report on the Americas*, 14–20.

Vitale, Luis C. 1996. "Cronología Comentada del Movimiento de Mujeres en Chile." In Zabrina A. Peréz and Luis C. Vitale (eds.), *Teoría y Práctica de la Escuela de la Formación Sindical Para Mujeres (Chile 1993–1996)*. Santiago, Chile: Buntstift.

Vogler, Justin. 2006. "Chile: The Rise of the Penguin Revolution." *Upside Down World* June 21. Available at <http://upsidedownworld.org/main/content/view/330/1/> (accessed on October 27. 2007)..

Washington Post. 2000. "Pinochet's Chile." Available at <http://www.washingtonpost.com/wp-srv/inatl/longterm/pinochet/overview.htm> (accessed on July 15, 2008).

Waylen, Georgina. 1993. "Women's Movements and Democratisation in Latin America." *Third World Quarterly* 14, 3.

_____. 1997. "Women's Movements, the State and Democratization in Chile: The Establishment of SERNAM." In Anne Marie Goetz (ed.), *Getting Institutions Right for Women in Development.* London: Zed Books.

_____. 2000. "Gender and Democratic Politics: A Comparative Analysis of Consolidation in Argentina and Chile." *Journal of Latin American Studies* 32, 3.

Welton, Michael R. 1993. "Social Revolutionary Learning: The New Social Movements as Learning Sites." *Adult Education Quarterly* 43, 3.

Wertsch, James V. 1985. *Vygotsky and the Social Formation of Mind.* Cambridge, MA: Harvard University Press.

Whittier, Nancy. 1995. *Feminist Generations: The Persistence of the Radical Women's Movement.* Philadelphia, PA: Temple University Press.

Wolcott, Harry F. 1999. *Ethnography: A Way of Seeing.* Walnut Creek, CA: AltaMira Press.

Wood, Elisabeth Jean. 2001. "The Emotional Benefits of Insurgency in El Salvador." In Jeff Goodwin, James M. Jasper and Francesca Polletta (eds.), *Passionate Politics: Emotions and Social Movements.* Chicago: University of Chicago Press.

Youngman, Frank. 1986. *Adult Education and Socialist Pedagogy.* London: Croom Helm.